The Music of

JEAN SIBELIUS

In the same series
The Music of Joseph Haydn: The Symphonies
The Music of Johannes Brahms
The Music of Johann Sebastian Bach: The Choral Works
The Music of Dmitri Shostakovich: The Symphonies
The Music of Wolfgang Amadeus Mozart: The Symphonies

Forthcoming
The Music of Gustav Mahler

By the same author
Hi-Fi for Pleasure
Bix Beiderbecke
Beethoven and Human Destiny
Living Forwards (autobiography)
Essays on Jazz
Music on Record (with Peter Grammond)
An Adventure in Music
Brahms: A Critical Study
Manuel de Falla and the Spanish Musical Renaissance

THE MUSIC OF JEAN
SIBELIUS
BURNETT
JAMES

WITH A FOREWORD
BY RAYMOND BANTOCK

Fairleigh Dickinson University Press
Rutherford · Madison · Teaneck
Associated University Presses
London

© 1983 by Associated University Presses, Inc.

Associated University Presses, Inc.
4 Cornwall Drive
East Brunswick, NJ 08816

Associated University Presses Ltd
27 Chancery Lane
London WC2A 1NF, England

Associated University Presses
2133 Royal Windsor Drive
Unit 1
Mississauga, Ontario, Canada L5J 1K5

Library of Congress Cataloging in Publication Data

James, Burnett.
  The music of Jean Sibelius.

  Bibliography: p.
  Includes indexes.
  1. Sibelius, Jean, 1865–1957. Works.   I. Title.
ML410.S54J33   1983   780'.92'4   82-24213
ISBN 0-8386-3070-7

Printed in the United States of America

For
JENNIFER BATE

Contents

Acknowledgements

My most grateful thanks are due to Mr. Kauko Karjalainen of the Foundation for the Promotion of Finnish Music, and the Finnish Music Information Centre, for invaluable help and co-operation, especially in the matter of supplying illustrations and for general information.

I am also most grateful to the following for permission to quote copyright material:

The page of score from *Rakastava* is reproduced by permission of Fentone Music Ltd. on behalf of the copyright owners VEB Breitkopf & Härtel, Leipzig.

The page of score from the opening of Sibelius's Fifth Symphony appears by permission of Edition Wilhelm Hansen, Copenhagen.

Editorial Note

This series is specifically designed to explore the sound *of each composer as his most distinctive feature, and, to this end, recognises the equally important role that recordings now play in musical life. Footnotes throughout the main text contain critical references to such recordings when it is felt that they clarify or highlight the composer's intentions. In the Appendix, these and other recommended recordings are re-grouped in a purely factual listing of catalogue numbers, performance details and any divergencies from the composer's expressed wishes.*

Since the aim of the series is to clarify *each composer's sound, particularly for the non-specialist, this approach should prove doubly rewarding: treating concert music as a living rather than an academic entity and showing the virtues and faults of its reflection through Twentieth-century ears.*

Foreword

[*Raymond Bantock is the second son of Sir Granville Bantock, the English composer, and Sibelius's most generous host and ardent champion in England. Sibelius stayed several times in the Bantock home either side of the First World War, the first time in 1905, the last in 1921. The second English visit was in 1908, when Bantock was rewarded with the dedication of the Third Symphony in the year after he had succeeded Elgar as Richard Peyton Professor of Music at the University of Birmingham. Mr Raymond Bantock subsequently visited Sibelius at Järvenpää and was received with reciprocal warmth and generosity — DBJ*]

Jean Sibelius was the greatest man I ever met.

I must have noticed him about the house during his early visits to our home, but my first direct memory of him is when I was in a restaurant near the Queen's Hall with my father, soon after 1912. Sibelius came in, and to my father's delight, joined us for a meal. I remember their amazement when the restaurant band began to play *Valse triste*. My father was devoted to Sibelius. I have no doubt that he insisted on paying for the meal, for, many years later, as I thanked Sibelius for entertaining me at his home he told me that, thanks to my father's generosity, he had never acquired any knowledge of English money.

My next memory of Sibelius is when he came to stay at our home in Edgbaston when my father arranged some concerts of his music in Birmingham, and receptions in his honour. His knowledge of English was never good, and it was reported to me that at one reception, whenever he was introduced to a lady, he said "I am pleased to make your connection." This must have been about 1921 because I was then up at Oxford. I remember Sibelius sitting in our drawing room, a massive, impressive figure who seldom spoke. It was arranged that we should visit Oxford and that I should show him round, Rosa Newmarch acting as interpreter. I remember well that when we were waiting on the platform to catch the train to Oxford, after standing very silent for a long time, he suddenly said to me in a voice that came straight from the heart, "Your father is so kind."

As a token of his friendship for my father, Sibelius dedicated his Third Symphony to him. When my father died in 1946, a society to foster interest in his music was formed. We sent a telegram to Sibelius asking him if he would honour us by being President of the Bantock Society. To our delight he immediately accepted.

Shortly afterwards, in the early 1950s, as it did not seem likely that Sibelius, who was then over eighty, would ever come to England again, I decided to visit him with my wife and eldest son, at his home near Helsinki. The arrangements were made by letter, and we were assured by the eldest daughter that our visit would be welcome, it being understood that this was something my father had always wanted to do.

So we went to Helsinki where his daughter called for us in a chauffeur-driven car. We drove north for about thirty miles through forests and past lakes, and eventually arrived at Järvenpää, where Sibelius lived in a beautiful house overlooking a lake in a small private forest. Sibelius would often walk in the forest, but always alone.

On our arrival, the composer came out, dressed in a large, white, double-breasted suit. He greeted us warmly, and served us with champagne as we reached the porch. We presented him with some gifts which were received with delight. We were then taken into the beautiful living-room looking out across the lake. There was a grand piano, a large bookcase on the wall, and pictures–all original paintings with a personal message. It was a warm welcoming house meant to be lived in, and not a show place.

During the morning we looked at his books and he fetched an autographed copy of Ernest Newman's book on Hugo Wolf. He also took me to a glass-fronted cupboard containing various treasures and gifts. He drew our attention to a cigar-holder given him by my father, and showed me with tenderness how he had put the cigar-holder next to the gold medal he had received from the Royal Philharmonic Society. When we were alone together later, Sibelius, with one of those warm sudden gestures so characteristic of him, took me in his arms and said, "I am so pleased to see you."

Later, he talked of modern music, which he said came from the head and not the heart. He told me that he often listened to broadcast music from London, and singled out one contemporary composer for special attention. "Fricker," he said, "has personality." He also spoke of Winston Churchill as "a great man." "He is a strong man," he went on, "I am not strong." I noticed that Sibelius suffered from a distinct tremor in his hands. I suspect that he suffered from a stroke of some kind after he had completed *Tapiola* - his last major work - and that that was why he subsequently did not compose any further symphony, nor conducted. I told him that I felt there was no need for a symphony after the Seventh because that work completed a perfect musical pattern which needed no continuation or embellishment. He seemed pleased with this.

During lunch I mentioned the Sibelius Society but he immediately brushed that aside and said, "Tell me about the Bantock Society." We feasted on strawberries, gathered from the garden by Madame Sibelius. However we did not see Sibelius's wife during out visit—she was, we were told, upstairs and not available because she spoke no English.

I noticed that Sibelius drank his wine from a large glass which he was obliged to hold carefully. During the afternoon, at my request, he gave me a portrait of himself, on which, with the help of a ruler to steady his hand, he wrote his signature.

Several times during the afternoon I suggested to Sibelius that it was time we left, but he refused to consider this till after tea. He really did his utmost to give us a reception of the kind that he would have given my father if he had ever been able to visit Finland. We were treated so affectionately. As we left the beautiful homely house and I looked back at it from the car, I felt sad because I knew we would never see the composer again. He was then 86 years old.

Years later I revisited Sibelius's home, but then, in 1965, it was to put flowers on the composer's grave.

RAYMOND BANTOCK

Introduction

When Jean Sibelius died in 1957, aged 91, it was widely held that the last link with the great tradition of European music was finally broken. It had been breaking apart for some time; one by one the giants of the old guard were falling; but this was seen as its final demise, the irreversible nemesis. There was truth in it; all the same, it was not an assumption to be made lightly. Births and deaths of traditions, epochs, historical continua, do not arrange themselves to the convenience of the calendar. It is always more a matter of signposts and indications in the context of the larger perspectives.

Sibelius was born into and grew to first maturity within that nineteenth century whose musical masters were Brahms and Wagner, and into which a new race of nationalists injected fresh and potent voices. At a glance, Sibelius appears to be one of them. Beyond doubt he was, to begin with at any rate, one of the leading nationalist composers, in both the broad and the narrow sense of that term: the character of his nationalism was at once domestic (i.e. inward-looking) and universal (outward-looking).

In the compositions of Sibelius the voice of the North became fully articulate in music. Before Sibelius, the North had spoken only in small, picturesque (even if recognizable and often charming) musical idioms, mostly folkish and entirely domestic. It fell, for the most part, into that category which caused Debussy to describe the music of Grieg, somewhat maliciously but not without a shaft of barbed truth, as "a pink bonbon stuffed with snow." Little of the innate power of the northern conscious- ness or the grandeur of the northern landscapes had found its way into the European mainstream and laid some lasting influence on it. There was no musical corollary of Ibsen. Grieg's own music for *Peer Gynt* defined the limitation.

Sibelius changed all that. He became, through his music and his personality, the embodiment of that consciousness and that landscape distilled in and through his profoundly Finnish mind. He eschewed folkery and the mere exoticisms of nationalism, and by the scope of his genius transformed his music into an expression of the consciousness of modern man in the emergent twentieth century. His orchestra shook with the gales and blizzards of the frozen plains; gaunt spectres from a far and legendary past haunted his woodwind figurations; heroic figures of mythology, their roots deep in the collective unconscious of his nation and hemisphere, struck hammer blows of brass chords.

So much has always been acknowledged. But it is not the whole story. It is perhaps in the end not even the most important part of it, for these elements in one form or another, depending on nationality and geography, are to be found in much of the art of the nineteenth century and after. Where Sibelius diverged from the prevailing ethic and aesthetic in his formative years was the way his mind and imagination were already probing into the future. From the outset he was beginning to discern the harsh features of the new century while others were still tending to bask in late romantic dream, the glow of a declining sun. Although he offered no direct challenge to musical tradition in the sense that Debussy, Stravinsky, and Schoenberg in their different ways challenged it, and as both Liszt and Wagner had begun to challenge it in their last works, Sibelius none the less can be shown to have represented less the end of a line, the culmination of a tradition, than the beginning of a new one. He was in fact, and seen in retrospect, the first complete manifestation of the twentieth century mind and consiciousness in music. That his technical means and roots were more or less traditional, and that he did not alter the language of music in its basic structures but simply used them in a new way, does not invalidate the argument. It simply postulates on the one hand the inner strength of the tradition* and on the other arises out of the way in which, for virtually the whole of the first half of its course, the twentieth century revealed no distinctive consciousness of its own but appeared essentially as a labouring extension of the nineteenth or an equally labouring reaction against it. Of

---

*As the late Professor Gilbert Murray once asserted, referring to Euripides, it is the strongest traditions that make the best rebels.

course, the turning point of centuries is simply another arbitrary division; all the same, there is such a thing as a nineteenth century consciousness, just as there was an eighteenth century consciousness and as there has slowly emerged a twentieth century one. In the crossing of the bar of the nineteenth and twentieth centuries there developed a kind of illusion caused by universal hesitancy and uncertainty, a sense of breakdown, a loss of traditional faith and values, of inner purpose and vitality in a period that produced, as outer evidence, two world wars of a scope that threatened the destruction of the entire fabric of European civilization without offering any real hope of regeneration.

Sibelius, like Mahler, stands at the crossroads of the modern world. And Mahler's popularity, his fashionable acclaim, rose at the same time as that of Sibelius declined. The reasons, superficially at least, were that the roots of serialism were discovered in Mahler, while the sound of Sibelius, by contrast, was seen as old-fashioned, monotonous, and provincial. Mahler was thus more in tune with the contemporary *Zeitgeist*.

The history of Sibelius's reputation in the good books of the cognoscenti makes an interesting and at times illuminating story. Raised to dizzy heights during the 1930s and 1940s (though Virgil Thomson's attacks in the *New York Times* began as early as 1940), he was subsequently cast into the depths no less violently. He was accused not only of unadventurous traditionalism but even more, on the basis of the finale of the Second Symphony and to a lesser extent of the Fifth, of undue optimism which ran against the contemporary grain. It is doubtful if any composer of like stature has ever been subjected to such a swing of fashion in so short a time. To many he must have seemed like Shelley's Ozymandias, and by the time of his death or shortly after should have declared: "Look on my works, ye Mighty, and despair!"

Yet it has to be remembered that this reputation was confined almost entirely to Britain, the United States, and Scandinavia. On the European mainland he was not appreciated at all; indeed, until well after the Second World War he was hardly known outside Germany, where he had achieved initial success before 1914, but was more or less forgotten afterwards in the crush of the new experimental and progressive music.

Reaction after the earlier extravagant praise was inevitable. Yet in one sense at least, the current of hostile criticism failed in its primary function. Instead of intelligent reassessment and revaluation, Sibelius became the subject of mere vogue criticism. This is something that is always liable to happen; but in the case of Sibelius it went so far in the opposite direction as to become at best ridiculous, at worst mindless.

On the other hand, even at the height of the fashionable reaction, records of Sibelius's music continued to appear and to sell in sufficient quantities to encourage commercial success. It is true that the recordings tended to concentrate on the more obviously popular works—the First and Second symphonies, the Fifth, and the better known tone poems, often used as fillups. Even so, a complete set of the symphonies with a number of tone poems appeared from Anthony Collins and the LSO on Decca during the 1950s, and a complete set of the tone poems came from Pye conducted by Sir Adrian Boult only a year or so later—that is, during the depths of the Sibelius depression. The Third and the Sixth symphonies, particular butts of some anti-Sibelians, tended to be ignored; but the Seventh held its own.

Indeed, Sibelius's larger international reputation was determined by the availability of recordings. Walter Legge's inclusion of the works of Sibelius in the HMV Society limited editions in the 1930s had an immediate effect. And Columbia had already brought out Kajanus's pioneering versions of the first two symphonies plus some smaller works, sponsored by the Finnish Government which, in a gesture of unusual enlightenment, contributed towards the cost, having already granted Sibelius a state pension. No British or American, and very few Continental governments would have dreamt of behaving in so eccentric a manner. Ever since then, Sibelius has been a strong favourite with recording companies, partly because he has attracted the attentions of most of the leading international conductors. To look at the Sibelius discography, past and present,* one would hardly guess that there had ever been a critical reaction.

There is no need to make excessive claims for Sibelius, as was once the custom. It is not necessary to argue that he was the greatest composer of his age, that he surpassed all of his generation and most before it. That is only to blur more of the outlines, to place him in another invidious position. He was not greater than Schoenberg, Stravinsky, Debussy, or Mahler; not necessarily greater than Elgar, Vaughan Williams, and Neilsen. And if we argue that as a symphonist he was largely superior to many who had come before him and others who were his contemporaries, that does not necessarily mean that he was a superior composer *per se*, only that he concentrated on one thing (or rather two, taking symphony and symphonic poem as

---

*See Appendix - Discography. Ideas on performance and interpretation of Sibelius's music have naturally changed since the pioneering days of Kajanus, Beecham, and Koussevitzky. Complete cycles of the symphonies have subsequently appeared from Maazal, Barbirolli, Davis, Bernstein, and Berglund; von Karajan has recorded most of them more than once. In fact Sibelius once said to Walter Legge, "Karajan is the only man who really understands my music: our old friend Beecham always makes it sound as if he had learned it and conducted it from a first fiddle part." (Elisabeth Schwarzkopf, *On and Off the Record: A Memoir of Walter Legge*. London: Faber & Faber, 1982). Nor have the Russians absented themselves, however much political history may at one time have militated against it: Rozhdestvensky, with Russian orchestra, has made several excellent contributions. Many other conductors have recorded one or more of the symphonies or collections of the tone poems. The Violin Concerto has never wanted for champions, apart from Heifetz's two outstanding versions. In fact, outside some of the inconsequential vocal or instrumental pieces, gaps in the Sibelius discography barely exist. Indeed the discography, in both quality and quantity is richer than for Tchaikovsky, and but a little poorer than for Beethoven and Brahms. The anti-Sibelius campaign is long since lost—or if it is not, then the news does not appear to have percolated through. Nor has it reached a new generation of conductors: Simon Rattle, for instance, has broadcast some symphonies in performances which show clearly how things stand.

separate categories, a distinction only in part sustainable), and did it exceptionally well. All Sibelius's other music is subsidiary to that; the product of his talent and his experience rather than of his genius.

What precisely constitutes that difference it is one of the tasks of criticism to find out. A second, and perhaps more important task, is to restore the overall perspective—this is particularly demanding in the case of the recently dead, if only because the perspectives are always shifting and may too easily turn into quicksands. If, as T. S. Eliot maintained, comparison and analysis are the tools of criticism, the critic still has to remember that he is dealing with living matter. He does not come to bury the dead. He is not a grave-digger.

Yet perhaps in another sense he is. If Hemingway spoke truly when he claimed that "a major art cannot even be judged until the unimportant physical rottenness of whoever made it is well buried,"* interment may well be a necessary part of the critical function, to separate that is the perishable from the imperishable. And it is both more difficult and more necessary in the case of one like Sibelius whose see-sawing reputation is still clear in the minds of the living. Yeats said it all in that last great poem, *Under Ben Bulben,* written a few months before his own death:

> Though grave-diggers' toil is long,
> Sharp their spades, their muscles strong,
> They but thrust their buried men
> Back in the human mind again.

---

*Death in the Afternoon. (New York: Scribner, 1932; London: Cape, Pan), p. 98.

Sibelius the Man

The idea still circulates that Sibelius lived a largely unadventurous life; that, cushioned from the harsher realities and necessities by a state pension, granted early in his career, his life thereafter was devoted to unmolested composition in the fastness of his house at Järvenpää outside Helsinki; and that he remained to a considerable extent remote and removed from the currents of the world around him, especially in his later years. A reasonably mobile youth is accorded him; but the subsequent impression is often of a formidable figure abiding in the forests of his Northern homeland. It is not dissimilar from the idea of Haydn, first making his way in a difficult world, then enjoying secure employment in a noble household, more or less immune from the tribulations and troubles of the larger world.

In both cases, the picture contains enough truth to deceive, enough error to distort.

Sibelius was born, on 8 December 1865, into a Swedish-speaking petit bourgeois family, the father a military doctor. He was the middle son of three children, the eldest a daughter, Linda, the youngest another son, Christian. The boy was christened Johan (Julius Christian) but was always known as Janne as a boy. The name Jean, by which he became internationally known as his career developed, seems to have derived from a seafaring uncle who used it for his convenience during his travels and prompted the composer to follow the useful example.

Although he was born into a reasonably established family, Sibelius's childhood did not pass without mishap. His father died of typhoid in 1867, leaving a mountain of debt and unpaid bills. In view of suggestions that Sibelius's silence during the latter part of his life was due in part to heavy drinking, it may be worth noting that his father's decline into debt and insolvency which led his widow into bankruptcy, was largely caused by a confirmed addiction to the bottle. His widow, Maria Christina, a woman of good and respectable family, did not wilt under the double blow of her husband's demise and an action for bankruptcy: she kept the family together and made her way back to her mother's home.

Despite the death and sad legacy of his father, Sibelius's childhood was happy and largely untroubled, thanks not only to his mother, but hardly less to his grandparents on both sides. He spent most winters with his maternal grandmother and his mother at Hämeenlinna, where his father had been stationed and his mother had been brought up. The feminine influence was predominant though not exclusive: his two grandmothers were widowed, but there was an Uncle Pehr, an amateur musician and successful businessman with whom young Sibelius formed a close relationship. In addition, most of the musical legacy to which he was heir, a legacy entirely amateur and never very strong, came from his mother's side. This is by no means unusual: a majority of musicians have inherited their gifts from their mothers.

The boy showed musical predilections from an early age. He was not a prodigy in the accepted sense of the term, and he was not a particularly fast developer. But he had unmistakable musical talent, though whether more than is normal for alert and intelligent children is not certain: in the case of the subsequently famous, there is invariably a good deal of special pleading and explaining after the event. Both Beethoven and Brahms have been held up as slow developers; yet each was certainly something of a prodigy in the executant field, and recent research has shown that the compositional development was not so far behind as is frequently supposed. What matters, however, is less the talent in itself than the capacity and determination to build upon it.

Sibelius not only had the basic talent for future development but he also showed early signs of wishing to develop it. He began to have piano lessons when he was nine years old (his sister also learnt the piano, and his younger brother Christian, the violoncello). However, his real allegiance was to the violin; even so, he did not commence lessons on that instrument until he was fifteen, when the bandmaster of the military establishment at Hämeenlinna, Gustav Lavander, took him in hand. Sibelius showed immediate aptitude, worked hard, and for some years cherished the ambition to become a peripatetic concert virtuoso. It proved, as an ambition, spurious and came to nothing; yet it left a twofold legacy—direct, in its influence on his writing for the solo violin in the D major Concerto and in other pieces; indirect in his exceptional mastery of orchestral strings. Whether or not he had or could have developed the talent to become a true international virtuoso of the violin is neither here nor there. It was not his destiny so to do and is therefore irrelevant.

While his interest in and capacity for music in general steadily advanced and developed, the young Sibelius was not clever or distinguished at school. That too is irrelevant; men and women of deep talent in a nonacademic direction are frequently less than brilliant with the standard school curriculum since they are seldom interested in it.

However, the young Sibelius soon came up against the familiar obstruction to offspring of the bourgeoisie: family objection to the idea of a musical career. He was accordingly required, while pursuing his musical activities for his pleasure, to undertake serious study towards a secure and "respectable" profession. (He was in good company: composers as widely separated in time and temperament as Gluck, Smetana, and Roberto Gerhard encountered and overcame parental opposition to a career in music.) He therefore applied himself to his books, passed his examinations, and in 1885 entered Helsinki University as a law student. But although he was prepared to be obedient and reasonably industrious in the matter of the law, at the same time he enrolled in the Conservatoire, continuing his violin lessons and adding harmony and counterpoint. He was only at the Conservatoire on a part-time basis; but inevitably more and more the law receded into the background while music became his primary activity. He had taken with him a string quartet when he went to the Conservatoire; but it was by no means his first composition. He had formed the habit of composing from early childhood, and the list of his juvenalia is quite impressive.

As usual, the contest proved unequal, and the following year Sibelius (like Edward Elgar a dozen years earlier) gave up the law for good and henceforth devoted himself to music.

It was now that the decisive influence came into Sibelius's life. He had entered the Conservatoire to study with Mitrofan Vasiliev, who was impressed enough to help Sibelius overcome the parental objection to a musical career. He then passed into the hands of Hermann Csillag. From all accounts both men were good and sympathetic teachers; but it was the Conservatoire Director, Martin Wegelius, who opened the future for the ambitious young student. Wegelius became virtually a paterfamilias to the young Sibelius, guiding him not only in music but treating him as friend and counsellor. As a teacher Wegelius combined strict observance of the law with imaginative understanding of latent genius. As Beethoven fell by happy chance into the artistic care of the excellent Christian Gottlob Neefe, Brahms with Eduard Marxsen, and as Delius came under the influence of the good Thomas Ward in Jacksonville, Florida, so Sibelius found one to set him upon his own road. Wegelius was neither a great musician nor an original thinker; but he was exactly the right teacher for Jean Sibelius at the outset of his adventure. Wegelius exercised restraint over his eager pupil's more fanciful ambitions, and at the same time instilled in him the rudiments of the art of composition in such a way that they took firm and unshakeable root in a propitious soil. Sibelius's later mastery owed much to Wegelius, just as Delius's owed much to Ward, though what each owed tended to be opposite—Ward revealed to Delius what he did not need from conventional academic techniques; Wegelius taught Sibelius exactly what he did require from the same source. (It is often the role of the good teacher to show the student what he or she does not need, every bit as much as the other way round: too much forced feeding can lead to creative impotence.)

The affinity between Wegelius and Sibelius went far beyond the normal student-teacher relationship; it soon became personal and intimate, the student staying in the master's private house and enjoying companionship as well as instruction. Wegelius at this time was a prominent figure in Finnish musical life, following Frederik Pacius, a pupil of Ludwig Spohr who had been among the most prominent figures in Finnish music through the nineteenth century, and rivalling Robert Kajanus, the conductor and composer who was later on to become Sibelius's close friend and colleague and the most distinguished conductor of his music. Just as Thomas Ward had urged Delius to continue and enlarge his studies elsewhere (in Germany), so Martin Wegelius recommended that his gifted pupil receive a state scholarship to enable him to study abroad. Initially there was a vague idea that he might go to study with Rimsky-Korsakov in St. Petersburg. The idea of Sibelius and Igor Stravinsky studying with the same master invites intriguing speculations.

However, he did not go to St. Petersburg and Rimsky-Korsakov, but to Berlin and Albert Becker—and, more important, the rich musical life of the German capital. He heard a great deal of the new German music as well as the German classics, notably Beethoven's string quartets and piano sonatas. And on the firm principle that you frequently have to travel far afield to meet your next door neighbour, it was in Berlin that Sibelius first heard Kajanus conduct his *Aino* Symphony, at a Philharmonic concert. The event had two important consequences: firstly, Sibelius made haste to introduce himself to Kajanus, thus launching a friendship and artistic collaboration that lasted, with one brief hiatus, until Kajanus's death in 1934; secondly, the *Aino* Symphony first turned his attention to the musical potentialities latent in the *Kalevala,* the Finnish national poetic epic which was to be a source of major inspiration for the rest of his life and the source of many of his most characteristic compositions.

Before he left for Berlin there was plenty going on for Sibelius at home in Finland, on both the musical and the personal planes. He continued to compose and began to receive congratulatory notices; but more important, in 1889, Sibelius's last year at the Conservatoire, Ferrucio Busoni arrived to become professor of piano. The two young men, contempories to within a year, soon struck up a warm friendship and discovered a mutual rapport both artistic and social. They exercised a cross-fertilizing influence on each other; and Busoni was later to become one of the early champions of Sibelius's music outside Finland.

During that year Busoni met and married the Swedish Gerda Sjöstrand, in Helsinki. At the same time, Sibelius was cultivating his friendship with the family of one General Järnefelt, a Finnish patriot and local administrator whose daughter he was soon to marry. The Järnefelts were high born and at first a trifle suspicious of the headstrong young bourgeois in their midst. But the three Järnefelt sons were all of an artistic disposition, the eldest, Arvid, a writer and amateur philosopher strongly addicted to the example and ideas of Leo Tolstoy; the middle son, Eero, a painter who had studied briefly in Russia; and the youngest, Armas, the well-known composer of a *Berceuse* and a *Praeludium* which have tended by their universal popularity to obscure his more substantial achievements in the field of choral and orchestral music. Armas, who also studied under Martin Wegelius, became an internationally famous conductor of symphony and opera.

Sibelius himself soon made friends with the Järnefelt brothers and would play many private recitals for violin and piano with Armas. He appears to have been greatly taken with the daughter, Aino, from the beginning; but being a young man of strong blood and various tastes did not formally declare himself or pledge his fidelity at once. It was not until after his return from Berlin in the autumn of 1890 that the engagement was announced, and the marriage did not take place until 1892, after the successful première of the *Kullervo* Symphony had established his position and his reputation.

In the meantime he had visited Vienna, where he continued his musical studies with Robert Fuchs and from time to time with the successful composer Carl Goldmark. All his life a good liver and enjoyer of the pleasures of the table and society, he found Vienna much to his liking in ways additional to the purely musical. Being young and impetuous, he indulged his taste, fell into new habits of extravagance, over drank, over spent, got himself into difficulties and out again, enjoyed the society (and from later accounts, often more than the society) of fair women. But his work was by no means neglected. His ambition to succeed as a concert violinist had not so much waned as submitted to the pressures of hard reality: it received a further, and perhaps final blow when he failed an audition to join the Vienna Philharmonic. If he had not failed that audition, there is no reason to suppose that the subsequent course of his life would have been in any way altered. He would simply have put a little more money in his pocket—or rather through the hole in his pocket.

His admiration for and understanding of Beethoven was further confirmed in Vienna; and the symphonies of Anton Bruckner seem to have considerably impressed him. This throws a little additional light onto Sibelius's early development. Martin Wegelius was and remained an ardent Wagnerian; and Bruckner was frequently dragged into the Wagner camp as the corresponding symphonist. Whether that assessment is just or relevant is for the time being beside the point; but there is no doubt that in retrospect there is a deeper relationship between the symphonies of Bruckner and those of Sibelius (especially the Sixth and Seventh) than may at first be suspected and than clearly was (or could be) discerned at the time of the latter's composition. Cecil Gray was not the only early commentator who claimed that the music of Sibelius shows no Wagnerian influence whatsoever. However, a later and perhaps wiser criticism has seen that the influence of Wagner, though never obvious, never anywhere near the surface, is still significantly operative at the deepest level. I shall return to this later when considering the question of Sibelius and opera; for the moment it is enough to state that the older idea of a Sibelius uninfluenced (uncorrupted some might say, or would have said a generation ago) by Richard Wagner is not to be sustained beyond the obvious and the superficial.*

Sibelius's own orchestral style was still not formed; hardly even embryonic. (He did compose an Overture in E major, which he passed over to Goldmark for comment and which Kajanus later gave in Helsinki.) But there were some songs and some more chamber music in which the true voice and tone of Jean Sibelius may at times be faintly heard. He was still finding his way—Brahms apparently liked some of his songs, although the letter of introduction he took with him to Vienna apparently failed to achieve a positive result and certainly never enabled him to study with the great man—and little was wasted in the line of musical potential. Good living and social extravagance did not divert him from his proper course. He seems already to have had an unusual capacity for living and experiencing, something that tended to increase rather than decrease as he grew older, though inevitably it changed direction and emphasis along the way.

More important, however, than all this listening and larking (as one may put it) was the way in which ideas for his first major works were slowly formulating beneath the surface, notably *Kullervo* and *En Saga*. Upon his return to Finland from Vienna in 1891 he immediately set about the serious and demanding task of completing *Kullervo*. (Though called a symphony, *Kullervo* is in fact a large choral/orchestral epic based on parts of the *Kalevala*.) Sibelius at first found it difficult to settle to hard work after the diversions of Vienna; but once he applied himself, the composition

---

*Gray further argues that "the art of Weber, of Berlioz, of Chopin, of Liszt, has had no effect, no repercussion, on that of Sibelius". This is palpably wrong, for, leaving aside the obvious fact that every composer must at least feel the repercussions of all his predecessors, the *Dante* Symphony of Liszt shows quite recognizable foreshadowings of the Sibelius sound and texture.

progressed reasonably smoothly. *Kullervo* was given its première on 28 April 1892, and was a marked success. Sibelius owed a fair part of that success to the fact that he had, by design or accident, contrived to do the right thing, at the right time, in the right place, in front of the right people. It was a period of patriotic upsurge in the wake of growing Russian pressure on the Finnish nation, with a number of writers and propagandists, with whom Sibelius was known to sympathize and whose aims and aspirations he shared, exerting a cumulative influence. In short, Sibelius had not only produced a significant piece of music; he had also struck a note, as Verdi more than once did in similar circumstances, that gave his work an impact and resonance beyond the purely artistic.

Kullervo contains many authentic Sibelius fingerprints, not least in the particular and unmistakably individual "tone" it established, both vocal and orchestral. It has its conventional, its nondescript passages, inevitably. It echoes the Russians here and there; Liszt elsewhere. But, and especially in view of the fact that it is his first major work and therefore his initial gambit with the orchestra on a large scale, it is far more remarkable for its authenticity of concept and execution than for its immaturities and short fallings. Everything about it, overall, suggests a major talent on the move. In some ways it stands parallel to *The Flying Dutchman,* in which Richard Wagner first found his true voice (and recognized it). In each case despite the alien elements and echoes, the vibrations of the composer's creative energy are revealed and are not to be mistaken.*

There, however, the parallel ends. If Wagner recognized and proclaimed the establishment of his distinctive art in *The Flying Dutchman,* and characteristically made the most of it, Sibelius, far from resting upon the laurels won for him by *Kullervo,* withdrew it from circulation the following year and never again allowed it to be performed during his lifetime. It had to wait until 1958, the year after his death, for a revival; fortunately, although he suppressed the score, Sibelius did not destroy it. It was preserved in the library of Helsinki University, and has now been accepted into the Sibelius canon.

The resurrection of *Kullervo* raises a number of interesting speculations. If it had not lain unperformed and virtually unknown for over half a century, what influence would it have had on the critical judgment of his work as a whole, especially during his lifetime and the period of his high reputation? More important, however, is the way in which *Kullervo* demonstrates that at the time of its composition and first production, although Sibelius's personal style was already formulated, the precise direction it should take was still undecided. In the light of *Kullervo,* Sibelius's art in 1892 might still have gone in one of several directions. It might, most directly, have evolved in the line of some form of music

---

*An even closer analogy is with Mahler's *Das klagende Lied,* except that Mahler returned later to his early work and presented a revised version.

drama. The handling of voices suggests that Sibelius could well have been led towards some form of vocal/orchestral response to Northern saga and mythology, whether inside the theatre or outside, as readily as towards the purely orchestral assumptions that in fact became the path he followed. In the light of some internal evidence and some hints dropped from his biography, the question cannot be dismissed out of hand or regarded as fanciful hypothesizing. To say that Sibelius after *Kullervo* might have followed the way of Wagner rather than Beethoven is grossly to oversimplify, even to distort; yet does help to pinpoint a necessary argument.*

Later in his life Sibelius said that he had often thought of revising and reviving the *Kullervo* Symphony but that its defects were too deeply ingrained to be corrected by revision or editing. Maybe, as the late Neville Cardus once argued (referring I think to Bliss's opera *The Olympians*), a flawed work of art has to go forth into the world and stand on its own legs, though bandy, and revisions usually amount to little more than being knowingly wise after the event. And was that another reason why Sibelius shied away from returning to *Kullervo*? Not only, not even primarily, because the amount of work required would have gone far beyond any accredited form of revision but because it reminded him of one road not taken, a possibility left largely unexplored? And farther still, did that too have some bearing on the long silence of the last thirty years of his life, after the Seventh Symphony and *Tapiola*? In other words, if he had followed the path of *Kullervo* as well as the other, would another and more fruitful potentiality have remained to him in the latter part of his life?

All this of course is unranged speculation. Yet it is given point by the way that, soon after the production of *Kullervo*, Sibelius was hard at work on an opera, *The Building of the Boat,* also based upon the *Kalevala*. It came to nothing and was soon abandoned; but it does indicate that Sibelius's mind at this period was running on lines not subsequently fully explored. This is a larger subject than relates simply to one period of his life and career: it will be dealt with more fully in the proper place; but it needs to be brought into preliminary focus here, as an essential part of the biography.

The immediate practical result of the *Kullervo* success was a commission from Robert Kajanus for an orchestral composition. This emerged early in 1893 as *En Saga* Op.9, possibly the first accepted masterpiece offered by Jean Sibelius who conducted the première himself on 16 February. As with several of Sibelius's works, it was withdrawn for revision after the first performance, but unlike *Kullervo* was not suppressed and has become one of his most popular pieces.

Other compositions followed, and in 1894 Sibelius paid his first visit to Italy. He returned via Bayreuth and attended Wagner operas, which greatly moved him. He tended afterwards to be somewhat cagey about his

---

*See Sibelius and the Theatre - p.113.

reactions to Wagner's music, perhaps because he had been more affected than he cared to admit. Whatever the outward influence on him of Wagner and the Bayreuth music drama, the internal effect was clearly far-ranging, though it is doubtful if the experience of Wagner affected his own operatic ambitions one way or the other.

Sibelius had already secured teaching appointments in Helsinki, at the Conservatoire and with Robert Kajanus's orchestral institute. In 1896, after the completion of the *Four Legends* (which include *The Swan of Tuonela,* originally planned as the Prelude to *The Building of the Boat*), he applied for a major post as Director of Music at the University. This was to have two important repercussions: first, it led to a quarrel with Kajanus; second, it was indirectly responsible for him being granted a state pension for life by the Finnish government of the day. Kajanus and Sibelius both entered for the post; Sibelius won, Kajanus appealed, and the decision was reversed. It appears to have been a familiar case of official muddle and incompetence; but it generated considerable bad feeling on both sides and ruptured a warm friendship and fruitful association. Luckily, the rupture was temporary, and within a couple of years the old cordiality had returned.

On the other side, the quarrel and its accompanying publicity helped call attention to Sibelius's personal position. He was already regarded as a national figure, not to say a national asset, and it was to relieve him of the necessity of undertaking hack work and encouraging him to continue independent composition untroubled by financial worry that the government awarded him a pension of 3,000 marks. In one sense, this was a piece of naïve optimism, for Sibelius continued his habits of high living, was a confirmed extravagant spender, did not know the meaning of economy and had no intention of learning it. He was in constant debt and made no effort to get out of it. No doubt the pension helped add a small stability at the bottom of the barrel; but any idea that it would meet his needs or curb his appetites was a long way beyond reality.

From one viewpoint, though, Sibelius's extravagances and demanding tastes had a beneficial effect. They obliged him to work to earn money. This, rather than the pension, helpful though that was, provided the real encouragement to productive work, apart from the artist's natural desire to work and create. The pension, however, remains a generous and civilized gesture on the part of society, despite the danger, not that it might encourage idleness, but the far deeper one that, as Graham Greene has argued, once an artist accepts any kind of privilege from state or society, his or her independence is threatened. It did not happen in the case of Sibelius; but the principle is a sound one.

His reputation was now secure at home, and as a new century approached it was beginning to filter through into the European mainstream. This began in Germany, where Breitkopf & Härtel undertook publication of his works, and for some time it was in Germany that he found most appreciation. His cause in France was advanced when he accompanied Kajanus and the Finnish National Orchestra to Paris for the Exhibition of 1900. However, he never made much headway with the French and even at the height of his later fame and reputation was regarded by them with a mixture of suspicion and indifference.

The previous year, 1899, had seen the successful production of the First Symphony, which virtually set the seal upon his future evolution, and his deepening involvement in Finnish national and political aspiration in the face of growing Russian oppression. He composed a good deal of overtly patriotic music, including some pieces written for a series of historic tableaux presented at a gala at the Swedish Theatre in Helsinki in November, ostensibly in aid of a Press Pension Fund but in fact a barely concealed patriotic demonstration. Much of this music did not survive the occasion for which it was written; but it also included his most famous piece, *Finlandia,* the finale and only surviving item from a suite entitled *Finland Awakes,* a piece that was seen as so ardently patriotic that it was condemned as seditious and was not allowed to be publicly performed in Finland for another six years, though it appeared several times in other countries under different titles. Other music from the 1899 gala became the *Scènes historiques,* in two suites Opp. 26 and 66, apparently separated by a dozen years in his catalogue but probably sharing the common origin.

Sibelius was of course no stranger to patriotic utterance. *Kullervo* itself, though not produced for a specific occasion, is full of national fervour; and the *Karelia* music derived from Sibelius's contribution to a pageant arranged by the students of Viborg University in 1893, while the *Four Legends* on the subject of Lemminkäinen promote similar feelings and ideas from a slightly different standpoint. Indeed, virtually all Sibelius's tone poems right up to *Tapiola* relate to his passionate concern for and deep response to the Finnish national consciousness and mythology.

After the successful tour with Kajanus culminating at the Paris Exhibition, which had included concerts throughout Scandinavia, Germany, and Holland, Sibelius's thoughts turned in the direction of a new symphony. At the suggestion of his friend and champion, Axel Carpelan, and sustained by a privately organized subsidy, he left Finland, going first to Germany, where he met Artur Nikisch in Leipzig, and then to Italy. A number of projects occupied him, but it was the symphony that demanded his attention to the exclusion of everything else, including a somewhat tentative idea of drawing upon Dante for a musical setting. He returned to Finland—via Prague where he had meetings with Dvořák and Suk—and worked hard to complete the symphony, which was premièred, after initial hesitations and false starts, in March 1902.

The D major Symphony behind him, Sibelius turned his hand to other tasks—among these the composition of incidental music for the play *Kuolema* by his brother-in-law, Arvid Järnefelt. A number of authors and composers have let best sellers slip through their hands without ensuring that they reaped the benefit, even severely practical and sharp-witted ones. Sibelius was one who allowed this to happen. In the *Kuolema* score lay the material that, rescored, was published as *Valse triste,* with *Finlandia* his most widely known piece: he sold it in haste for a pittance and lived to regret his lack of foresight for the rest of his life. It was subsequently played all over the world in every conceivable arrangement (and a few inconceivable ones) and would have netted him a fortune in royalties, something he would greatly have appreciated, since he was, as always, deeply and risingly in debt.* The other survival from the *Kuolema* music was an amalgamation of two items to make the quietly beautiful *Scene with Cranes*.

Debt or no debt, Sibelius now launched into property ownership. He bought land some twenty miles outside Helsinki and built himself a fine house, at Järvenpää. Here he lived with his family for the rest of his life: in later years it became a place of pilgrimage for his admirers and of prodigious hospitality.

To this period, alongside some smaller works, belongs the Violin Concerto in D, by no means his best large-scale work but the one in which he distilled all that remained of his youthful ambition to be a concerto virtuoso. A peculiar feature of Sibelius's career as a composer is the way in which so many of his works were first presented in a form very different from the final one. He probably "tried out" more compositions on the public than any other composer of like stature. There is no problem of editions, as with Bruckner; but if one runs a finger down the list of works, the number of dates of original composition followed by a later date of revision is remarkable. And sometimes a revision is masked by the absence of a preliminary date, possibly because it is not known, or not recorded. In a man of such obvious intellectual stature, such assured compositional technique, and such sturdy determination, it can hardly have been a case of lack of self-confidence or uncertainty of aim, especially since it carried over into the later stages of his active career in some cases. Many composers, notably Brahms, have destroyed youthful or other works not to their satisfaction; and as many have revised or recast work in progress before issuing it for public performance. But few have proceeded quite as Jean Sibelius did, and on so many occasions. It is a minor anomaly, and if it is not of surpassing importance, it still invites speculation.

The Violin Concerto was one of the larger works subjected to this curious process. It was composed in 1903, presented in Helsinki having failed to meet its original promised date (but there is nothing remarkable in that), was then withdrawn for revision and given its official première in Berlin in October 1905, Karl Halir taking the solo part, Richard Strauss conducting. It is possible that in this case the reason for the presentation then withdrawal was perfectly simple: he needed money in a hurry and

---

*Unlike Wagner, Sibelius did not assume that the world owed him a living, even if he sometimes used it for his convenience. All the money he borrowed was repaid.

finished his work in haste. It would be an adequate explanation if it had not been repeated too many times in quite different circumstances.

Besides the official première of the Violin Concerto with its distinguished conductor in Berlin, further evidence of the progress his reputation was making in Germany can be taken from an invitation from Busoni to conduct the Second Symphony at one of the latter's New Music concerts, also in Berlin. It was largely because of this and a commission to compose incidental music for a production of Maurice Maeterlink's *Pelléas et Mélisande* at Helsinki's Swedish Theatre, that Sibelius postponed for a year a projected visit to England, where his reputation was also beginning to become established . He finally made the trip in November (1905) and was overwhelmed with hospitality, especially from Sir Granville Bantock, which provoked his famous remark that during the whole of his stay he "never made the acquaintance of English coinage." The visit was a great success all round. Both the First and Second Symphonies had been given in England that year, the Second by Hans Richter, and other pieces had prepared the way ahead of him. Henry Wood agreed to give the première of the Third Symphony in 1907 (it was not in fact ready until a year later and was then given by Bantock, to whom it was dedicated). The major works of the following year were the tone poem (one of his best), *Pohjola's Daughter*, and the incidental music for Hjalmar Procopé's *Belshazzar's Feast*, a score which contains several example's of Sibelius's gift for evoking a particular, if alien, atmosphere. Another small outcome of the year 1906 was the Dance Intermezzo *Pan and Echo* (revised 1909).

Now came a crisis. During the earlier part of 1908 Sibelius experienced increasing pains in the throat. He was obliged to seek medical advice, and a tumour was diagnosed. It was thought to be nonmalignant; but a series of operations were necessary for its successful removal, and for several years afterwards he lived in fear that it was not done with and that the malady would finally end his life. In 1909 he made a second trip to England, was again warmly welcomed, conducted his own works, heard a great deal of the music current in London at the time, including Debussy's and Elgar's, and made the first acquaintance of several more prominent English musicians. While in England he completed his only important piece of chamber music, the string quartet *Voces intimae*. He wrote, especially in youth, a good deal of chamber music of one kind or another: some of it survived but little is of much consequence and hardly any is now performed. Another work of 1909 was the tone poem *Nightride and Sunrise,* another of his best and most characteristic, and also that year the sombre *In Memoriam*.

Although he appears to have recovered, he still lived in the shadow of potentially fatal illness. He had given up aspects of his lifestyle which meant much to him, including drink and tobacco. All the same, he continued to travel, to compose, and to conduct. Yet the internal crisis was central and had a direct bearing on all he did and wrote, not only now but for some years to come.

It was in 1909 that he started work on the Fourth Symphony, the work above all that contains the concentrated essence of Sibelius's style and method, the purest distillation of his total ethic and aesthetic. The symphony is built upon the tritone which in medieval times was known as *Diabolus in musica* because it undermined the tonal order, the *si contra fa* which challenged the perfect fifth, the musical equivalent of God. For Sibelius, living as he did at the time in the dark shadow of mortality, *Diabolus* was no doubt more than *in musica* only. But whatever of that, there is no doubting the Fourth Symphony's nature and character. The shadow of death, real or imagined, has the effect of concentrating the mind (as Dr. Johnson observed in a different context); and if the mind in question is that of a composer, it may concentrate the productions of that mind also.

The Fourth Symphony took two years to complete, during which time some other small compositions and more travels intervened. The symphony was given its première under Sibelius's own baton in Helsinki on 3 April 1911. It was not well received, largely due to its uncompromising nature; and it continued to puzzle and provoke hostility when it was played in Germany, America, and England.

With both the experience and the composition of the Fourth Symphony behind him, Sibelius was now at the height of his powers, and despite the enigma, the symphony appeared in many places, was more and more recognized as a major voice in contemporary music. In 1912 he was offered the professorship of composition at the Vienna Imperial Music Academy. He turned it down; but the offer influenced the Finnish government in a decision to increase his state pension. In 1913 he intended to return to England for a third time and to produce a new work for the Cathedral of Gloucester. He did not write it and did not come to England, though the Cathedral had its more than adequate recompense of presenting the first performance of *Luonnotar,* one of his subtlest, most completely original, and most totally individual works. The same year also produced a small masterpiece, the tone poem *The Bard.*

A clutch of pieces, small in dimensions but rich in quality, is gathered round the Fourth Symphony. They include *The Bard* and *Luonnotar*, plus the suite for strings, tympani and triangle, *Rakastava*. Then came a visit to America and a commission from Carl Stoeckel for a choral work for the Norfolk Festival. Instead of that however, what appeared was another orchestral piece, the tone poem *The Oceanides*, one of the very few Sibelius tone poems not based on the *Kalevala* and Finnish mythology.

America delighted Sibelius, as Sibelius seems to have delighted America. As on his first visit to England he had been generously entertained by Granville Bantock, so in America he was no less generously accepted by Carl Stoeckel and his wife. It is not recorded if he did or did not make acquaintance with American currency (the likelihood is that he did), but everything went well for him in every department. He received an honorary degree from Yale University, was greeted everywhere as a famous man and a major composer, generally disported himself in his fame, and saw some fine opportunities for the future. He entertained ideas about planning a massive concert tour as soon as possible, seeing, like so many before and after him, the USA as a kind of touchable gold mine for the restitution of fallen fortunes and the building of new ones. His brother Christian was apparently also a dedicated accumulator of debts, and Sibelius told him that such a tour through the States would "pay off both your debts and my own." For Jean Sibelius too the summer of 1914 was almost what Henry James in another connection called "a monotony of fine weather."

*

It has often been said that the history of Jean Sibelius during the second half of his life is the history of his compositions. What is nearer the truth is that it is the history of two World Wars and a long silence.

Sibelius went to America in May 1914. Two months later the fatal shot was fired in Sarajevo; and the next month, Europe had plunged into the cauldron. By that time Sibelius was back in Finland; but any ideas that he could retire to Järvenpää and devote himself to quiet composition while the world around him indulged its taste for masochistic bloodletting were soon dispelled, if they had ever seriously been entertained. Finland was not immediately involved in the war; but world wars do not stay long away from anyone's door. It knocked on Sibelius's in several ways.

To begin with it hit his pocket, always a sensitive spot. With Germany locked in war and Finland nominally neutral but closely linked to Russia, Sibelius's transactions with the publishers Bretkopf & Härtel became at first uncertain and later broken altogether. So he lost a major part of his income through royalties. He began his association with Hansen in Copenhagen; but there was no quick way of recovering the lost revenue; and in any case, performances of music became inevitably rarer and for new music rarer still. He was thus obliged to compose in a way that would help boil the pot. It has frequently been asked why Sibelius composed so much inferior music, salon pieces and the like. The answer is for much of the time quite simple: he needed money. At this period and in these circumstances, he was in even more urgent need of it; so it is not surprising that during these years he wrote a great many pieces which could be sold for a reasonably quick return. It is not necessarily that these pieces are bad in themselves; they are often quite good of their kind. Unlike Elgar's salon and other similar pieces, those of Sibelius do not appear to have been produced simply because he liked them (as Elgar did); not are they linked to his major compositions, musically, in the way Elgar's were. The cleavage between major and minor Sibelius is generally much larger than that between major and minor Elgar.

There are several close correspondences between the careers of Jean Sibelius and Edward Elgar. Some are obvious, like the penchant for churning out trifles and the enrollment of the patriotic muse—though even here is a difference: Elgar's national and state occasional music was celebrating a triumph achieved and already on the wane though not everyone knew it: Sibelius's was dedicated to a struggle very much of the present and to an aspiration projected into the future. Yet the linkages remain and should not be ignored. Beyond that, there is the question of contemporary idiom. On the surface, the music of Elgar and Sibelius has little in common, either in form or in content. But in art, surfaces often conceal more than they illuminate. The two men went their different and individual ways; yet at the beginning it was less clear cut. Lay *Kullervo, Karelia, En Saga,* the first two symphonies and the Violin Concerto of Sibelius alongside the associative works of Elgar, say the two symphonies, *Cockaigne, Pomp and Circumstance,* perhaps *Caractacus,* and although the chronology is different and at no significant point are the methods the same, there is no doubting that it all comes from a similar period in musical and European general history; that the warp of consicousness involves the same evolutionary cast. But what if Sibelius had been born into Victorian England and Elgar in nineteenth-century Finland? The roles reversed invite a number of possibilities, especially in view of the existing musical and career parallels.

It is of course nothing new or strange for composers who live at the same time and period to reveal particular parallels and correspondences. Yet it has a significance of its own here, if only because of the separation of both England and Finland at the time from the European musical mainstream. The differences of course are no less marked, the most obvious being in the matter of response to a religious faith.*

Despite the amount of vocal and choral music he composed, few if any major composers left less related to religion or the liturgy. Manuel de Falla, in Spain, did not write one liturgical or specifically religious work; but the whole of his output was in the profounder sense religious, an act of faith and a thanksgiving to God. Elgar, a Roman Catholic in a Protestant country, wrote much, if not most of his music out of the exigencies of faith, though seldom from a sectarian viewpoint. But with Sibelius there is barely a hint that religion, at least in any organized sense, even existed. (There is a small piece for solo voice, chorus and organ, issued as *Musique réligieuse* in 1927 but not published: it is not in any case notably religious music.)

---

*The "English connection" goes a good deal farther and deeper than a career parallel between two men who put their respective countries' music into the European mainstream, one for the first time, the other as a resuscitation. The impact of Sibelius on English music was wide and varied: direct in the case of Vaughan Williams and Bax, both of whom dedicated their Fifth symphonies to him, less direct with such as Moeran, Walton, Rubbra and others.

This does not perpetuate the old idea of Sibelius as a musical primitive and pagan. Far from being a primitive, Sibelius was in fact an extremely sophisticated composer who could also be a very clever one when he needed to be; an elemental composer, maybe, but that is not the same thing. And as for paganism, that is an invidious term anyway, one not to be idly bandied, especially in a scientific rather than a specifically religious age. Delius was the true pagan among contemporary composers.

The First World War, however, hit Sibelius harder and more hurtfully than in his pocket. He was approaching his fiftieth birthday and he prepared for it, consciously or unconsciously, by setting to work on a new symphony, the Fifth. The birthday arrived and was celebrated with national festivities and rejoicing—and with the première of the symphony.

Thus far everything was in order. But it did not stay that way. Of all Sibelius's major works, the Fifth Symphony is the one that went through most public revisions, most premières and repremières. It was also the most affected and interrupted by extraneous circumstances—war and personal worry.

During these years of the 1914-18 war Sibelius lived in fear of his health and of a recurrence of his throat trouble, which before it was rid of entailed more than a dozen surgical operations. At the same time he endured great and increasing hardship from the conditions of war. Although Finland was not involved in the war as combatant, she was deeply involved by circumstance. The Russians and the Germans squabbled over Finnish territory; and after the Russian Revolution in 1917 the Bolsheviks moved in and Sibelius's home at Järvenpää was molested. In 1918 civil war broke out, and Sibelius, as known patriot and supporter of the Finnish national cause, was in actual and immediate physical danger. Things became so bad that he was obliged to seek sanctuary with his family in Helsinki where his brother was senior consultant at a psychiatric hospital. But this proved no safer: the Communists soon moved in and commandeered the hospital; food was desperately short, most other amenities virtually nonexistent. Then the Germans came and there was a furious bombardment before the situation eased, the Bolsheviks were driven out, Finland proclaimed an independent republic, and Sibelius was able to get back to work.

Such was the physical background to the emergence of the Fifth Symphony. After the first performance in 1915, Sibelius withdrew it for revision. It was presented again in 1916; and withdrawn again, this time for three years. The final version, the one we now possess, appeared in 1919 the structure radically refashioned, the original four movements made into three, the first in particular now a kind of telescoping of first movement and scherzo, all most cunningly and skilfully executed.

The war ended, a kind of peace returned. Sibelius resumed his normal life at his house at Järvenpää. Through the first half of the 1920s his life continued much as before. He composed; occasionally he travelled. In

1920 he received an offer of professor of composition at the Eastman School of Music, which he first accepted but never took up. In 1921 he made his third and last visit to England where he picked up his old friendship with Busoni. According to Sir Henry Wood, the two of them painted the town red every night and generally made life difficult for concert promoters and other mundanely interested parties. It was typical: Sibelius never lost his verve for life or his taste for high living; and in Busoni he found a more than willing partner. It was also a valediction: three years later Busoni was dead without the old friends and comrades meeting again. In 1923 came a concert tour of Norway and Sweden, the première of the Sixth Symphony under his own direction, and a further trip to Rome and Italy. In 1924 he completed the Seventh Symphony; in 1925 *Tapiola;* and in 1926 the incidental music to a Copenhagen production of Shakespeare's *The Tempest.* The year 1929 saw the publication of his last opus in the catalogue: the Three Piece for Violin and Piano Op. 116, a hardly perceptible flick of the ageing titan before he withdrew forever into the fastness of his old age and the forests of his native land, a retreat leading to his virtual elimination from the active musical scene, a dark forest of the mind as well as of animate nature.

That is the impression; those are the bare bones. From 1930 onwards, his age then 65, his creative calendar is a blank; not a single other entry until his death twenty-seven years later. The sudden break was, and remains, inexplicable. The years 1923 to 1926 were highly productive, with two great symphonies, the finest of all his tone poems, *Tapiola,* his most extensive and masterly contribution to the theatre with *The Tempest* score, plus a large quantity of minor music. His sixtieth birthday, in December 1925, was celebrated with even more festivities and national rejoicing than his fiftieth had been. He was honoured at home and abroad. To all outward appearances he was sound in mind and happy in home and work. There was no hint that his powers were in decline. By all normal computations at least another decade of creative work lay before him; more if he continued in good health. Yet the rest is silence.

A number of explanations have been advanced to explain the mystery; none satisfy. Increasing addiction to alcohol has been proposed as one major reason: unable to dry out, he dried up. Alcohol may have been a contributing factor; but no more. All his life he had imbibed liberally, yet the high productivity of his middle years and the eventual length of his lifespan suggest that it did not do him all that much harm. In any case, the way in which he was able at the time of his first throat surgery, around 1908, to give up all drink and tobacco for a decade indicates that he was slave to neither, certainly not a confirmed alcoholic.

It may of course not be necessary to look for devious explanations and external causes at all. Perhaps it is not even a mystery but a simple case of creative honesty: he felt that his life work was completed, that he had given what he had to give of himself and thereafter he preferred the dignity of silence to old age's garrulity. Arnold Bax used to say towards the end of his life that he had retired, "like a grocer." In the case of Jean Sibelius it could also have been as straightforward and uncomplicated as that. Yet there is clear evidence that Bax's mental and physical powers were already showing signs of disintegration, and indeed he died not long afterwards, his age still short of seventy, whereas there is no such evidence with Sibelius.

That his powers were inhibited by a feeling of increasing isolation from the post-1918 musical world also seems unlikely. Although he maintained an alert interest in all that was going on in the musical world to the end of his life, Sibelius was never one to chase any devil of contemporary fashion by the tail. He was always a man who went his own way and paid little attention to the gaudier exuberances of critical flag-waving and transitory "movements." His well-known remark, relating to the Sixth Symphony, that while other composers gave the world highly spiced cocktails, he offered "pure cold water," suggests that he knew very well what he was about. It is true that in the conditions prevailing in the wake of the First World War, his music had lost most of its appeal in Germany where, as elsewhere in mainland Europe, experimentalism and new ideas were turning the older musical world inside out; but he was held in the highest esteem in other parts of the globe, notably Scandinavia, England, and America where many of the leading conductors and critics set themselves to champion his cause. No: neither reaction against him in certain, admittedly influential quarters, nor the overfulsome praise of some critics, notably Cecil Gray and Constant Lambert (who may inadvertently and with the best intentions have placed him in a slightly false position as the great master of modern music, fit to be mentioned only beside Beethoven as a symphonist) can seriously be held to account for his lack of major composition after the Seventh Symphony and *Tapiola*.

No doubt, like all true artists, Sibelius experienced periods of self-doubt and some disillusionment. But that need not destroy the creative powers, rather it is a constituent and energizing part of them.

Elgar too suffered inhibition and disillusionment after the First World War. But for him the collapse of the old world was more than a case of musical reaction. Firstly, the laureate of the twilight of England's imperial splendour, he had seen it all perish, along with virtually a whole generation, in the mud and carnage of the Somme and Passchendaele, an experience not shared by Sibelius who, although he had lived through hardship and privation, civil war and riot, saw his country emerge not to debilitation but to new nationhood. Secondly, nearer the end of his life and career, Elgar had a personal reason for withdrawal when his wife, the inspiration for his entire career, died. Yet before his death in 1934, there were indications that Elgar's creative powers were beginning to revive. In this respect, though outwardly similar, the cases of Sibelius and Elgar do not run in direct parallel.

Vaughan Williams, though of the same generation, in similar

circumstances, continued to compose without inhibition in a style not dependent upon fashion or "modernity" through a second world war and into another new age.

It is thus evident that the reason, if there is one, for the long silence from Järvenpää lies not externally but internally. And here it may open a line of enquiry by referring back to *Kullervo*. Sibelius concentrated his creative work into symphony and symphonic tone poem, and it is possible that after the Seventh Symphony and *Tapiola* he found that these two particular veins were worked out. But his concentration on them had been so close, so exclusive that he had left himself with no other options open. Yet if he had followed the line of *Kullervo*, perhaps into some form of vocal/orchestral music drama, or had continued his practice in youth of writing chamber music instead of leaving the single string quartet, *Voces intimae*, he might have found the way ahead less blocked.

In the earlier part of his life, Sibelius, like Wagner before him, believed that music could only fulfil itself entirely in conjunction with words. He either abandoned that idea or decided not to act on it. If Sibelius had followed up his own lead in *Kullervo* he might have left, from his maturity and even into his old age, major choral/orchestral work, either singly or in a series, in the form of a great Nordic epic paralleling in his own terms Wagner's *Ring*, and almost certainly derived from the *Kalevala*, not to the exclusion of symphony and symphonic poem but alongside both.

All this is speculation. Yet such is the mystery that whenever we approach Sibelius and try to see him whole and in the round, some obstinate questioning of the riddle seems both necessary and inevitable. And indeed, the speculation is not simply abstract: it has its beginning and end in a seedbed of fact—*Kullervo* at one end, the mythical Eighth Symphony at the other. *Kullervo* was never followed up, and Sibelius seems to have had a curious inhibition about returning to it. At the other end, the failure of the Eighth Symphony to materialize suggests that perhaps that particular mine really was worked out.

With most composers who lived long and produced major work to the end, the total catalogue shows considerable variety—chamber music, orchestral music, instrumental music, vocal music, all jostling together and each category producing a body of important compositions. It is rare that a composer who works one vein only produces copiously and over a long period (it is perhaps rarer that a composer works one vein anyway). The exception is of course Verdi, who wrote opera with much vigour and dedication through his youth and maturity, then after a pause, produced two masterpieces, *Otello* and *Falstaff*, in extreme old age. Wagner might seem to constitute another exception; but Wagner's music dramas are so all-embracing that they appear to comprehend any number of different genres in themselves. Wagner, as usual, constitutes not so much an exception in itself as an exception within an exception, or probably more accurately, an exception outside an exception. In any case, it is almost certainly easier indefinitely to extend an operatic career than a symphonic one, the more so if the symphonic career itself has been devoted to extending and subtlizing the essentials of the genre rather than simply repeating them.

It is usually argued that one of the characteristics of Sibelius is his fecundity, yet in no other composer of consequence is the division between his permanent and his ephemeral work so marked and so numerically balanced on the side of the latter. By comparison with Richard Strauss, Stravinsky, Schoenberg, or Vaughan Williams among his contemporaries or near contemporaries, he was not prolific with music that matters. And several others, like Mahler, produced a great deal more major music in a much shorter time. The great length of Sibelius's life tends to distort the picture.

Haydn at the end of a long active life turned to choral music. It was not a new departure for him; but, and this is the point, he picked up a genre he had worked spasmodically before and produced his late master-pieces in the last Masses, *The Creation,* and *The Seasons.* He had left all lines of communication open. Beethoven at the end turned to string quartet, and had he lived would almost certainly have done the same, on all internal evidence. Brahms, who lived twenty-five years less than Sibelius but died at roughly the same age when Sibelius ceased to compose, produced in his last years beautifully mellow chamber music, leading in style out of his earlier work, and those sad, reflective, deeply original and forward-looking piano pieces which bore fruitfully upon both Schoenberg and Webern. (Schoenberg's essay, "Brahms the Progessive" is still insuffi-ciently known and understood.) Yet Sibelius, who had achieved so much, exerted so potent an influence in certain quarters, suddenly broke off composing, almost in mid flight. If he did not, like Achilles, sulk in his tent thereafter, he never again came forth to join combat. It is as though Beethoven had suddenly ceased to compose in 1812, with the *Archduke* Trio and the *Emperor* Concerto, both works of serenity and calm unassertive power achieved through personal fulfilment. No "third period."

So we return to the Eighth Symphony. Apart from the fact that it does not exist (and may never have existed,) it had a curious history. Many times it was announced, promised, promulgated by word if not deed. Many times expectation ran high; many times it was disappointed. Through the 1930s rumour proliferated. As late as 1945 Sibelius wrote to the conductor Basil Cameron that "my Eighth Symphony has been 'finished' many times." But yet again, no symphony. Sibelius was, despite some impressions to the contrary, a man of wit and humour, perfectly willing to pull a leg or two, or tweak a too inquisitive nose, and visitors to Järvenpää who tried to extract precise information would usually get a mildly snide reference to the old Scandinavian proverb, "One doesn't sell the bearskin until one has shot the bear."

Touché: but the question still remains.

After Sibelius's death, his family announced that there were no unpublished works to come. For some time the musical world was inclined to take that statement with a sniff of suspicion. But indeed there was no Eighth Symphony; with Sibelius there were not postumous works. (*Kullervo* is not really an exception as the score was known to be in the library of Helsinki University, even if it remained unpublished and unperformed.)

It seems that in some strange and largely inexplicable way, the music that Sibelius did write precluded the possibility of his writing any more. For the time being it is perhaps best left at that.

*

By the time the Second World War broke out Sibelius was confirmed in both silence and reputation. Again, Finland was not directly involved at first, was not one of the combatant nations. But in 1940 Soviet Russia, having previously annexed the Baltic states of Latvia, Lithuania, and Esthonia, launched a full scale military invasion of Finland that was as vicious and unmerciful as it was incompetent. Obviously the Russians expected a quick kill, possibly an immediate capitulation as a large and powerful nation hurled its force at a small and nominally weak one. But Finland was small only in size and not at all weak in spirit. The result was a savage war of heroic resistance against what should have been (and were, but only after prolonged struggle) impossible odds.

As in the first war, Sibelius again endured great hardship and privation. There were reports at one time that he had suffered death or serious injury, either from air attack or artillery bombardment. Fortunately they were untrue; but he still underwent severe discomforts, to say the least. He received many offers of sanctuary abroad, but declined them all without hesitation, as one would have predicted. In the inevitable peace treaty which followed in 1941 when Russian brute strength had finally overwhelmed Finnish defence, Finland was obliged to yield territory, including part of Karelia.

In many ways it was a typically Sibelian situation, linking back to the years of his youth when Finland's struggle for national independence and resistance to Russian oppression had inspired many of his best early compositions. Yet this time, although he made a radio appeal to America and a fund-raising postage stamp was issued bearing his head and the words "I need your help," he did not break his vow of musical silence. No patriotic utterance in music came from him, despite the urgency of the hour and the profound feelings it must have caused him. All the same, he symbolized to a world already locked in a larger combat, the heroic stand of a small nation against the bullying of a large one, itself in the circumstances of the time an exemplar of all that the worldwide conflict was fundamentally about.

Unhappily, it did not end there. As the major war progressed and the Finns coddled their resentment against Russia, Hitler's attack on the Soviet Union gave them the opportunity to seek revenge and retake the lands that had been forcibly appropriated in 1941. Instead of a campaign of limited objective, the Finns drove deep into Russia itself, taking temporary advantage of the German pressures, though at first they stopped at the original 1939 boundaries, an act that materially assisted the Russians in the defence of Leningrad by leaving the western shore of Lake Lagoda free as the only supply route open when the city was cut off on all other sides. However, the subsequent retreat of the German armies left Finland once again at the mercy of the forces of war, and once more she suffered greatly.

And of course Sibelius too suffered yet again with his country. There was considerable chaos and impoverishment. At the war's end Sibelius was reported to be in want. What seems more probable was that he was suffering the restrictions and deprivations of postwar uncertainties and reorganizations, which were universal rather than purely personal. But the reports brought forth new offers of help from many parts of the world, which left Sibelius in no doubt of his standing among civilized people. And Sibelius himself was an essentially civilized man who believed deeply in the virtue of civilization. In spite of—or may be because of—his deep responsiveness to and understanding of nature, often at its most hostile and inimical, he was in no sense an artistic or existential primitive. *Tapiola* in particular demonstrates the inherent hostility of animate nature expressed through a completely sophisticated technique. He once said that the great nations of Europe had endured in a way no savage could have stood: "I do believe in civilization." He had reasons personal as well as general for such a statement.

The war over and a gradual return to a kind of normality enabled Sibelius to resume his elected lifestyle. His eightieth birthday had been overshadowed by the harsh events of war and its inevitable disorganization; but his eighty-fifth and then his ninetieth were occasions for even more national and international celebrations than the earlier ones had been. Political as well as artistic leaders paid him tribute and sent him gifts.

Towards the end he began to look frail and gaunt; but his mental powers seem to have been little impaired; nor was his great gift for hospitality. For years Järvenpää had become a place of pilgrimage, both for tourists and for colleagues from the musical and artistic worlds. As his age increased, it was inevitable that the number of visitors fell away; but those who were permitted received the warmest of welcomes and the utmost in attention. Being a fundamentally shy man who hated fuss and publicity, the ever increasing swarms of tourists caused him some annoyance and had to be restrained. But no one who gained access to his villa, Ainola, came away disappointed or short changed. For a composer mostly associated with "cold" music, full of the echoes of frozen wastes and icy winds, all who met him became immediately aware of the warmth of his nature and the richness of his humanity. Honours showered upon him as the years passed; but it did not turn his head or distort his personality. And he was a great and voluminous correspondent, letters always answered, friends and colleagues never forgotten or neglected. In his younger days he was also a great talker: most who knew him agree that he could not only drink but talk most of his guests under the table.

Even the longest years must one day come to an end. On 20 September 1957, Sibelius had a cerebral haemorrhage in the afternoon and died during the evening, while Sir Malcolm Sargent was directing the Helsinki Symphony Orchestra in a performance of, appropriately, his Fifth Symphony. And it was appropriate: if the Fourth Symphony is music to live by, on the principle that we live by wounds and not by solaces, the Fifth is fair music to die to—a final garnering and gathering of vital energy, a gesture of affirmation, the trumpet sounding on this side in anticipation of that on the other side.

Both Beethoven and Byron died in the midst of thunderstorms; but Sibelius had, in a manner of speaking, already trumped most of the aces of Nature.

*

A man's public image does not always accurately reflect his innermost personality. It is so in the case of Jean Sibelius. By reputation austere, aloof, given little to rejoicing and less to mirth, the impression is reinforced by a superficial acquaintance with his music. And to a certain extent it is true; at times in his life he does seem to have been very much a personal embodiment of his most rigorous and austere works. But that is only one side of the picture and in the end not the most important one. The legend persists; the man remains elusive.

There is an idea that Sibelius could not easily relax; that he could not, or would not, smile; that he was seldom, even when caught off his guard, to be found warming his hands at the fire of life. Arnold Bax left an illuminating vignette in his own autobiographical *Farewell My Youth,* which contrasts the earlier with the later Sibelius between, that is, 1909 and 1936:

> "The massive, bald-headed titan of the latter year, suggesting an embodi-
> ment of one of the primeval forces that pervade 'Kalevela', can at a whim
> transform himself into a purveyor of farcical fun and Rabelaisian joviality.
> But the earlier Sibelius gave one the notion that he had never laughed in his
> life, and never could. That strong, taut frame, those cold steel-blue eyes,

and hard-lipped mouth, were those of a Viking raider, insensible to scruple, tenderness, or humour of any sort.

An arresting, formidable-looking fellow, born of dark rock and northern forest, yet somehow only half the size of the capricious old Colossus of to-day."*

The dates are significant. By 1909 Sibelius was under the threat of his throat ailment, thought at first to be cancer. And it was the time of the genesis of the Fourth Symphony, that key work for Sibelius in so many different ways. We know that in his youth Sibelius was anything but the tough Viking of 1909 in Bax's description. He was a high liver, convivial, definitely a rake, easily recognizable as the father of the later capricious old Colossus. Perhaps in 1909 a complex of harsh experiences, inward and external, that brought him to the brink of the Fourth Symphony had become uppermost and taken temporary charge. Robert Layton states** that "the unsmiling Nordic giant with features of granite . . . is a myth." But Bax's impression is from personal contact; it is unlikely to be pure fancy. The overall deduction is that Sibelius was a more complex and varied human being than has generally been supposed and as may be assumed from some of the more obvious features of his compositions. Works like the Sixth Symphony, *Rakastava, Luonnotar,* several others of the highest quality, reveal him as a man and artist of great subtlety of mind and delicacy of feeling, far removed from the popular misconception of him as a kind of chest thumping Tarzan of the North, or as a Nordic giant forever bawling and brawling and savaging the orchestra with seismic upheavals, windy roarings, and uncouth belches from the heavy brass–at best a musical merchant in ice packs and old bones. All these latter ideas of him have been current at one time or another, especially during the years when reaction set in and the stock of his reputation plummeted, even before his death brought the predictable reaction.

Opinions differ, impressions diverge when it comes to assessing his personality and essential character. That is inevitable and unavoidable: it is also necessary. The only reliable way through, however, is via his music. That too is inevitable and necessary.

---

*Arnold Bax, *Farewell My Youth,* (London: Longmans, Green & Co., 1943) p.61.
***Sibelius* (Dent "Master Musicians"), p. 24.

1 : *Symphonies and Symphonic Poems up to 1910*

Before embarking upon a systematic discussion of Sibelius's music it may be useful first of all to clear the ground of a few unnecessary obstacles. Among these is the loose and largely inattentative use of the terms *classical, romantic,* and *sonata form,* three means too often employed by criticism to signal the existence of an aesthetic or metaphysical (or both) proposition and then to evade it. Though each may have viable meaning within a specific context, they can never be used as blanket expressions rendering all subsequent definition redundant, as though that is any or all of them are fixed and rigid in abstract determination, as kinds of categorical imperatives independent of time, place, and circumstance. *Classical* and *romantic* are in a sense relative terms, dependent upon the particular situation of their application.* *Sonata form,* being a directly musical hypothesis, comes into a different category; but it too is not fixed and finalized, once and for all: at its deeper levels it has a malleable, evolutionary significance.

If *classicism* implies precision, economy, and objectivity, and *romanticism* emotion, imagination, and subjectivity, that does not take us very

---

*cf. Charles Rosen, *The Classical Style,* (London: Faber & Faber, 1971, 1976) far. Kierkegaard declared, "Subjectivity is truth," and if classicism does not also embrace a form of subjectivity, the implication must be that classicism is little more than formalism and has no existential relevance. One might say that classicism is the corollary of academic criticism and romanticism that of existential criticism; but that does not get us very far either. It postulates an aritificial division and implies an erection of meaningless barriers. If classicism is equated with intellect and economy and romanticism with emotion and extravagance that is simply to push the salient, and largely superficial characteristics to the perimeters. The truth is that neither classicism nor romanticism are mutually exclusive categories but, like baroque*, permanent constituents of the human consciousness, not the unique manifestation of a particular period or era. Every artist, whoever or whatever he or she may be, is a mixture of the classic and the romantic. The precise definition, if it exists at all, is not a matter of absolute division, but of bias and emphasis. To argue that romanticism implies a total reaction against intellect is the same as to say that classicism is an expurgation of all emotion and imagination, both propositions so ridiculous that no one can begin to take them seriously. Anyone who cannot discern the colossal intellect at work in Wagner's music dramas (or on a different scale in the best works of Liszt and Berlioz) is incapable of understanding anything, as little as those who see not emotional content but only form and pattern in Bach, Haydn, or Mozart. That, of course, is to push to extremes; but the implications of an argument are as important as its immediate causes. Beethoven, as always, faces both ways: the vindicator of form in music and the ultimate repository for the expression of feeling and spiritual value.

Every style or creative direction that passes into history reaches its high point, then tends to become degenerate and corrupt. Thus the classicism of the eighteenth century became mere formalism and the romanticism of the nineteenth became little more than emotional wallowing. But that does not invalidate either, in their proper historical context. What it does invalidate is all attempts to ressurect either in specific terms outside the period of its creative relevance. Thus classicism today cannot mean what it meant in the eighteenth century, and romanticism in the twentieth century has little to do with what would have been understood by the term in the early years of the nineteenth. Both have passed into history: evolution has advanced and cannot be reversed.

It is therefore necessary to bear all this in mind when referring terms like *classic* and *romantic*—and in a more precisely musical sense *sonata*

---

*"Baroque is not a phenomenon of the seventeenth and eighteenth centuries alone. It is a recurrent phenomenon in art: the ancient Greeks had their baroque. It is something that always happens when two main factors coincide in point of time—a great store of technique, transmitted and personal, and an enormous heightening of sensibility." - Ernest Newman in "Bach and Baroque," *Sunday Times,* 14 January 1934, reprinted in *From The World of Music* (London: John Calder 1956), p.110.

form—to Sibelius. Emanating as he did from the late nineteenth century and picking up, both consciously and subconsciously the sensitive antennae of the emergent twentieth, he cannot be treated as though he belonged to another time or another place by the unconsidered use of terms from a different historical context. This is not invariably the case with every composer of the same generation. We may call Elgar "romantic" without serious distortion because Elgar (and also both Delius and Rachmaninov) remained by nature and temperament locked in a kind of time warp. Despite certain technical responses to the new century and its ways, these and their like were *romantic* in the sense in which that term could legitimately be understood in relation to both their time and their creative natures. But such terms cannot be applied to Sibelius, except by inference and through redefinition. They have their uses, as all general terms have. They will be used hereafter; but not as labels or as side-stepping substitutes for the argument.

The essential Sibelius is to be found in the seven symphonies. Everything else is to a greater or lesser extent a by-product of that central achievement. Whatever may be said about the symphonic tone poems, and there is much to be said for they represent an important side of his creative faculty, the guiding principles are to be found in the symphonies. The source of the initial inspiration may be different; but the fundamental principles of composition are invariably determined by the symphonic origin. This is by no means always the case with composers who leave a number of symphonies in the body of their catalogues. Indeed, in the period of Sibelius's lifetime it is nearer to an exception than a rule.

The symphonic poems of Sibelius occupy a particular place in the totality of his output. Into them went matter not appropriate to symphony proper. Thus he avoided one of the worst pitfalls of nineteenth-century symphonists—precisely that of confusing symphony with symphonic poem and therefore producing a series of hybrids. For Sibelius the distinction was clear and always observed. During the 1930s, he discussed these matters openly with Walter Legge. He said then that his symphonies "are music conceived and worked out in terms of music and with no literary bias"; and he then added that his symphonic poems were "a different matter" and "are suggested to me by our national poetry." Subsequently Ernest Newman took the question up in one of his weekly articles for *The Sunday Times* (30 December 1934) as part of the whole business of *pure* and *impure* music.* Newman argued that the distinction is basically a false one and that a

---

*All music is to a greater or lesser extent both "pure" and "impure"—pure in the sense that every musical work (every work of art of any kind, one might say) has to obey certain objective laws of its own constitution, however primitive or elementary; impure since no artist works in a vacuum and nobody can produce work totally unaffected by personal temperament, emotional colour, racial consciousness, or the collective unconscious. The totally objective is as much an illusion as the totally subjective—and as undesirable.

musician's creative activities are the result of a process in which "the whole man thinks." This, of course, is indisputable; and it is just as true of Sibelius as of anyone else, whatever the exact context. All the same, and from his own point of view, it is not difficult to see what Sibelius was driving at.

An earlier indication of Sibelius's thinking came in his celebrated meeting with Gustav Mahler when Mahler visited Helsinki in 1907. On that occasion Sibelius said that what he admired in the symphony was "its style and severity of form, and the profound logic that created an inner connection between all the motifs." To which Mahler retorted, "No, no! The symphony must be like the world. It must contain everything."*

So as early as 1907 Sibelius knew precisely where, symphonically speaking, he was going. He also knew where he was not going. Those words make it clear that for him the symphony does not "contain everything"; it has strict laws and logic of its own. And what it does not contain, but what it was also necessary for him to express in his music, went into the tone poems. It is this absolute clarity of his thinking and the uncompromising nature of his genius that enabled him to see the way through the woods while so many others lost time and direction confusing two separate musical issues. For while Newman's argument that in everything he does "the whole man thinks" is true, it does not mean that the whole of him must be deployed in every direction all the time.

Thus the symphonies and tone poems of Sibelius run side by side throughout this career in a kind of interactive parallel, each throwing light on the other, right up to the last tremendous parallelism of the Seventh Symphony and *Tapiola*. Thus although aim and intention may differ between symphony and symphonic tone poem in Sibelius, there is never stylistic dichotomy: the creative mind and the hand that serves it remain the same. It is not always so, at other times and in other places. Thus both Sibelius and Newman are vindicated.

Sibelius was thirty-four years old before he wrote his First Symphony: like Brahms before him, he bided his time and addressed himself to that

---

*The distinction between Sibelius's and Mahler's idea of the symphony remains. Somewhere between stands Carl Neilsen, hardly known or recognized outside his native Denmark during the high noon of Sibelius's fame and reputation, but later "discovered" during the 1950s. Nielsen's symphonies avoid the extravagance and all-embracing quality of Mahler's, but have little of the logical cogency and intellectual severity of Sibelius's.

Mahler's view brings to mind the character in André Gide's novel *Les Faux-Monnayeurs* ("The Counterfeiters") who declared, "police notwithstanding I would like to put everything into my novel." James Joyce was similarly inclined when writing *Ulysses* a decade earlier. This kind of heady excess was very much in the air in certain artistic quarters either side of World War I. It was something that Sibelius stood against, though not quite in the way it once appeared.

major task only after careful preparation. By the time he came to it, in 1899, he had behind him not only his long and deliberate years of apprenticeship with their severe attention to matters of form, mostly in chamber music, but a number of orchestral compositions in which his emerging genius was able to gain experience and advantage. The ground was properly prepared. *Kullervo,* though a large and extended work and called "symphony," is not totally symphonic in the sense Sibelius himself came to understand it, so that its resurrection after his death did not alter the original perspective. In so far as *Kullervo* pointed to the future it stood nearer to *En Saga,* which immediately followed it, than to the First Symphony. It pointed, that is, in the direction of symphonic poem rather than symphony.

The E minor Symphony at once established Sibelius's symphonic premises. It strikes, to be sure, a strongly national-romantic note, externally. But what it assumes of that is already under sentence, has almost become by then a part of history, both musically and existentially. It is not only in the intellectual grasp of symphonic form and structure and the underlying severity of style (despite a certain outward luxuriance of instrumentation and melody) that the late romantic tradition with its sense of melancholy and nostalgia, the "sunset glow," is challenged; it is even more in the firm, unshakeable foundation tones, the barely concealed menace of many of its thrusting themes and the insistently pounding rhythms which have the effect of purging both easeful lyricism and autobiographical melodrama. Notwithstanding some external aspects carried over from the departing century, the First Symphony of Sibelius is not retrospective: the A flat Symphony of Elgar, written nine years later, is essentially backward-looking, a kind of spiritual and aesthetic apotheosis of an age and an aspiration already past its zenith; Sibelius already looks forward to the rough ride awaiting European man in the coming century.

We need not read too much into the uncompromising materials out of which much of this remarkable opening symphony in the series is built. Not yet is the full Sibelian ethic and aesthetic formulated and made articulate. All the same, the plain fact remains that here, at the outset of his career as a symphonist, the embryo of nearly all that was to come is already established. What is to follow will be more in the nature of a deepening and enrichment of complexity and a fining down of method than any radical shift of course and direction.

The suggested correspondences with Borodin, even Tchaikovsky, are partly coincidental, partly a matter of contemporary affiliation, much in the way that German music of the Brahms-Schumann period and association tends to have a related tone and texture without necessarily sounding the same, or cribbed. Yet with Tchaikovsky there is really no link at all. Everything in Sibelius runs contrary to Tchaikovsky's conception and practice. There is perhaps a small hint of similarity in a few generally Russian ways of writing for the orchestra, soon to be expurgated. I suspect that the E minor Symphony* of Sibelius originally derived its Tchaikov-skian associations from its occasional tendency to indulge in seductive melody and from the apparent willingness of its tunes to respond to the kind of interpretation frequently accorded to Tchaikovsky. The time signatures and some melodic curves suggest here and there, out of context, a Russian dance, even a valse, and sound quite pretty thus played.† But look at the melodies themselves; look further, to the wind and string figurations that surround them and to the nature of the rhythmic founda-tions which underpin them, and the Tchaikovsky correspondences recede to insignificance. True, this is the most opulent of all Sibelius's sym-phonies in point of melodic and orchestral indulgence. Sibelius here permits himself a gratification of the sensuous, which, later, he eschewed with some determination. In the finale he actually projects a big, round, pot-bellied tune, though there is still a dark and sinister aspect to it, as in the movement as a whole which Sibelius (unusually) described as "Quasi una fantasia." And the slow movement, Andante, contains in its main theme one of the few instances in Sibelius, certainly in the symphonies, of a melody charged with a kind of romantic melancholy and nostalgia, a passing regret perhaps for a day that is gone, or fast going. Yet even here, as in the big tune of the Finale, the particular character is confined to the strings; around and through it woodwind chatter and brass interject in a manner unmistakably Sibelian and effectively dispelling all trace of senti-mentality. The tune of the Andante itself

has been likened to a folk melody; but whatever its origin, the tone is that of early Sibelius.

The relationship with Borodin is more subtle and far-reaching. Whether because he had actually studied Borodin's scores or because he reached similar conclusions by a different route, Sibelius began from principles first outlined by Borodin. The latter had many years earlier been

---

*It was even hinted at one time that the relationship between Sibelius and Tchaikovsky lay in that both had written symphonies in E minor, a comparatively rare key—until somebody remembered that Brahms had written one too.

†An exponent of this type of Sibelius performance was the late Paul Kletzki—Leonard Bernstein just manages to avoid it. On the other hand, Paavo Berglund seems to go almost too far in the opposite direction, deliberately declining the romantic gambit. Maazel brings it off admirably. Kajanus in his 1930 recording has the final imprint of authority.

experimenting with a form of that preliminary thematic fragmentation that was to become so marked a feature of Sibelius's maturing style. Also, a number of structural principles now associated with Sibelius were in fact originated, if in a more basic form, by Borodin. How far Borodin exercised a direct influence on Sibelius, or how much it was a case of similar ideas being in the air at a certain remove and striking two otherwise disparate creative minds in dissimilar contexts, is hard to say. What seems clear is that the minds of Borodin and Sibelius tended to move on conjunct courses at a distance of some forty years. This becomes still more apparent in the Second Symphony, and is still to be noted in the Third.

Echoes of Beethoven likewise appear in the First Symphony of Sibelius, most notably in the rhythmic motivation of the drums in the scherzo and the motion and impulse of the winds parts in the first movement following letter G and before Y. But these are only echoes. The real legacy of Beethoven lies not in any obvious external features picked up by a magpie ear, but in the profound implications of inner motivic unity. Sibelius showed that he was totally aware of this in the conversation with Mahler in 1907; but it is already operative in the E minor Symphony. In fact, this unity of motif is a characteristic of the true classical symphonic style; it is there in Mozart and Haydn, but it was Beethoven who brought it to its farthest reaching and most imperative operation, just as he established the principles of structural motivation in works like the Fifth Symphony and the first *Rasoumovsky* string quartet through a process of compression by foreshortening and the cutting out of all bridge passages and episodes. It is from this point of view that Sibelius may justly be called the legitmate heir of Beethoven as a symphonist. It is not a value-judgment (which is something else and is also important,) but a rigourously musical one.

In the First Symphony motivic unity is already a leading principle. How conscious or subconscious, or how much of both it was, cannot be accurately defined. It is closely involved with the permanent question of the relationship between the conscious and the sub- or unconscious in every act of creation. Sometimes, when a particular relationship between themes or motifs or some other aspect of a work is pointed out to a composer, he will reply that it was not intended and is simple chance. But that in itself is a kind of coincidence; it is analagous to G. K. Chesterton's point that the critic's job is not to tell an author what he knows about his work but what he does not know and cannot know, what will "make him jump out of his boots."*

---

*Introduction to Dickens's *The Old Curiosity Shop*.
   Sibelius himself, when a thematic correspondence in the Fifth Symphony was pointed out to him, is reported to have replied that he had not intended it and it was "pure coincidence." But this does not mean very much. In the act of creation, a composer, novelist, poet, painter, becomes

The E minor Symphony begins with twenty-eight preludial bars for solo clarinet, accompanied for the first sixteen by a soft tympani roll, then unaccompanied. This is hardly a slow introduction in the old sense: it provides a kind of opening gambit, a stepping-stone to the main matter of the movement, yet one in which the seeds of germination are carefully sown*. It also established in symphony another primary aspect of Sibelius's style and method, his penchant for spinning long asymetrical, nonstanziac melodies. He had already written the most famous of all these in *The Swan of Tuonela*, originally intended as the prelude to the unfinished opera, *The Building of the Boat.* This was not exactly the same thing as Wagner's *unendlich melodie* but was obviously related to it. Sometimes, as here, the melodic unfolding contains within itself the germ of what is to come; sometimes, as with *The Swan,* its function is complete in itself.

Because of its intrinsic importance, this preludial melody is worth quoting in full:

Clarinet in A

totally immersed in the work in hand, his or her mind obsessed by the material so that internal cross references are always liable to crop up, whether consciously recognized or not. It is precisely this, when brought to his attention, that will make him "jump out of his boots."

*Even at this early stage Sibelius's method has nothing in common with an *idée fixe* or with the "cyclic form" used by Elgar after César Franck. It is the beginnings of a genuinely organic way of thinking and composing, the linking and interlocking of motifs nearer to the cellular evolution of living organisms.

The more one studies this, the more significant does it become. If *a*) promotes *b*), then *b*) promotes *c*) and later on *c*) becomes

Flutes in thirds

which is nothing less than the "second subject." In addition, a similar figure often motivates the appearance of the main theme of the movement, and the whole may even be seen to contain by implication the triplet that rounds off that subject. The true symphonist wastes nothing.

A bar by bar breakdown of any symphonic movement would destroy rather than illuminate it, because dissection reveals the how but not the why and therefore misses the essential point. As Schoenberg argued, what matters is the final result; the means are the composer's business, not the listener's. All the same, once the clue has been given, it is often remarkable how much the ear picks up and identifies without further precise definition. The intellectual and aural satisfaction received from a Sibelius symphony, beginning to end, is the result, to a large extent, of the inner logic and unity of his technique.

The first movement of the E minor Symphony is the most interesting, the most potent, and the most organically structured. The Scherzo has much of that rhythmic propulsion that is one characteristic of Sibelius, one of the elements that helped give him popularity during the 1920s and 1930s when in the musical world the vogue was that rhythm is all. Perhaps the Finale, and not only in its pot-bellied big tune, does not avoid the vulgar, as the Andante does not altogether avoid the sentimental. None the less, the symphony as a whole is more remarkable for its original traits than for its commonplace aspects and conventional features. Even the organic first movement has its uncertainties of touch; yet the whole is notable for its profoundly indented fingerprints. The urgencies of rhythm, the successive accumulations of sheer physical force, the interlocking of thematic "cells" within all four movements; above all, the sudden gusts of brass tone rudely disturbing the chattering and scampering woodwind thirds, and the great ostinato organ points deep in the bowels of the orchestra—all these, and more, proclaim unmistakably the hand of Jean Sibelius.

All may not be blazing originality. Sibelius was still working his way towards his mature symphonic style. But the combination of ingredients—some Borodin, some Beethoven, and a great deal of original

Sibelius—is enough to stake out the ground and point in decisive directions.

In point of form, the E minor Symphony shows no major innovation; only an individual use of established methods and an avoidance of most of the pitfalls and extraneous ingredients of the typical late nineteenth century romantic symphony. In the Second Symphony, however, Sibelius made an important advance along the road of structural innovation as well as further confirming his unique tone of voice in large scale composition. Indeed, in the D major Symphony virtually every ingredient of Sibelius's mature symphonic style and method is expounded. In the later symphonies all he really did was to modify or further develop some aspect of the Second. The extreme precision and economy of the Fourth can be seen as a distillation of the essence of the symphony, a kind of abstraction by paring to the bone. Even the apparently new element of the modal and polyphonic techniques of the Sixth and Seventh symphonies can be traced back to embryonic origins in the earlier work.

Indeed, it goes back a good deal further than that, to the *Four Legends* of 1895, to the two well-known numbers,* *The Swan of Tuonela* and *Lemminkäinen's Homecoming,* originally written in the mid-1890s, where two of the salient principles of Sibelius's overall style, in both symphony and symphonic poem, are first adumbrated. Just as *The Swan* is an early and outstanding example of his way of writing long weaving asymmetrical melodies, often launched by a single held note or a repetition of the same note producing a similar effect, so *Lemminkäinen's Homecoming* is a no less outstanding demonstration of his habit of building from scraps of thematic nuclei, a kind of mosaic technique over irresistible forward-thrusting rhythmic repetitions, a powerful accumulation of fragments into a resplendent final unity. These were to remain among the most significant of Sibelius's methods, with increasing subtlety and inner complexity, throughout his career. Both are implicit to a greater or lesser degree in certain passages of *En Saga,* the first of his fully developed symphonic poems, alongside the tonal freedom and extended range of modulation that is another feature of his maturing style. But it is in the two *Legends* that they are given initial clear cut definition.

En Saga in fact, in its two versions, throws much light upon Sibelius's growth to full artistic manhood. It is a work that had strong personal implications. In it Sibelius reconciled those personal and national elements of his style, hinted at, but not achieved, in *Kullervo*; the two finally fused

---

*The other two—*Lemminkäinen and the Maidens of Saari* and *Lemminkäinen in Tuonela*—remained for a long time in manuscript and largely unperformed. The complete sequence has, however, been recently recorded by Sir Alexander Gibson, Okko Kamu and Eugene Ormandy among others. *Lemminkäinen in Tuonela* in particular is more than fit to stand with its more famous companion pieces. As well as *The Swan of Tuonela*, the second number, *Lemminkäinen in Tuonela*, contained material carried over from the unfinished opera *The Building of the Boat*.

into a preliminary whole which was to be consolidated and extended in all his subsequent works. The first version, written in 1892 and given in public in 1893, predates the First Symphony; but the revision, in which form it is always heard today, dates from 1902, contemporary that is with the Second Symphony. Thus *En Saga* crosses the barrier in Sibelius's creative evolution between the first two symphonies, throwing its light both ways.

In the first version *En Saga* was somewhat loose in form, haphazard in structure. Its main constituents of melodic expansion and freedom of tonality were in the revised version somewhat curtailed without being fundamentally undermined. This is in accordance with Sibelius's later practice. The tonal range, from A minor to E flat minor, with the centre held in C minor and E flat major, was preserved; but the whole was considerably tightened and cross-braced in the revision. One feature however remained: the clarinet solo, between U and W in the published score, relating to the first theme but also containing embryos of other thematic material, presaged in reverse the opening clarinet solo of the First Symphony in which the germination of the principal material is enunciated. The relationship between the two, symphony and symphonic poem, can hardly be overlooked or misconstrued.

One of the most remarkable features of *En Saga* is the way in which a virtually conventional language is used to wholly individual ends. When Mahler condemned the music of Sibelius as little but "hackneyed clichés," he missed the point. It is true that much of Sibelius's music, (and in particular his earlier works to which Mahler referred, since the famous meeting took place in 1907) is based on established methods and an academic use of the orchestra. But Sibelius had already learnt to call upon these methods and techniques in the service of a wholly individual voice. In other words, he had already learnt how to use the established language in a new and original manner.

But Sibelius was firmly entrenched in a national as well as a personal security. He had his solid background, both ethnic and individual. He was in no sense working in a vacuum. He had learnt his craft in the centres of European music; and he felt at home there. Mahler, by contrast, had no firm centre, either national or personal: he always felt himself "thrice homeless . . .an intruder everwhere." Always the outsider, Mahler felt himself obliged to work in a contrary direction, away from the firm centre. It was a matter of psychology as much as of musical tenacity.

The Second Symphony initiates several symphonic processes of increasing importance. It is all very well using a specific technique on a comparatively small scale; it is quite another to refer it to the heart of symphonic structures on a large scale. Yet this is precisely what Sibelius did, and with the most positive and telling effect.

It has sometimes been proposed that in the first movement of the D major Symphony Sibelius begins with thematic fragments and only in the recapitulation allows the full melodic content to emerge. But this is a very shallow and short-sighted view: if it were totally true it would in any case make a nonsense of the inner principle of organic growth in a symphony. It cannot be substantiated unless one is bogged down in textbook ideas of sonata form which apply only for a kind of indolent convenience and have little relevance to the actual music under discussion. While it is plain fact that the movement is constructed out of thematic nuclei, it cannot be argued that they resolve ultimately into a recognizable melodic structure in any accepted sense—unless, that is, it is maintained that, taking the long overall view, the broad melodic expansion of the finale was germinated in the thematic chippings of the first movement. That is a tenable hypothesis, harking back to the way in which the initial theme of the Finale of the First Symphony was also generated in the opening clarinet solo of the symphony's first twenty-eight bars. But if that is true, as on the long-range assessment it is, then it has to be accepted that the entire symphony, in all its four movements builds out of the fundamental elements of the highly original and nonreferable first movement. To approach this first movement from the basis of rule of thumb textbook sonata form is to miss its essential element of genuine creative power. It can, like much else, be made to conform to that conception; but only at the expense of distorting its true and original significance.

The procedure adopted by Sibelius for the opening movement of the Second Symphony is not only different from, but in several important aspects in opposition to the conventional idea of sonata form. It may perhaps best be described as a form of nuclear method of composition, by which the primary unit of thematic energy rather than the theme itself is the determing factor. Though a natural melodist, Sibelius does not invariably begin with broad melodic statements, at least in his larger and more complex designs. And even when he does it is not with straighforward terminal melody according to classical precept but with that form of asymmetric unwinding that is his particular hallmark. More often he works from handfuls of thematic nuclei which by a subsequent process of organic growth and fusion evolve into complete structures. And this, of course, is virtually a reversal of the standard classical procedure where a theme or group of themes is first stated (exposition), then subjected to some form of extension or analysis (development), finally to be restated in their original form or a variant of it (recapitulation) within a general pattern of tonal and harmonic evolution. But this is not Sibelius's way, even when, as in the first movement of the Third Symphony, he appears to be running closest to so-called sonata form in what is imagined to be the classical mould.

Thematic fragmentation is not, however, an accurate description of Sibelius's approach to symphonic structuring. Fragmentation implies the break down of an already existent whole into a greater or lesser number of random parts. But with Sibelius the whole does not exist until its basic parts, its active nuclei, have been brought together and placed in a new and unexpected relationship. Nor does this apply to thematic (i. e. potentially melodic) material only: it is no less—and inevitably since the constituent parts do not exist in isolation—operative in the handling of rhythmic and harmonic nuclei, so that the totality of the musical thought-process only becomes apparent after its primary ingredients have been expounded in detail.

Borodin had begun to work from similar premises some forty years before Sibelius; and it is probably not without significance that Borodin was a chemist by profession and would therefore be familiar with organic growth in natural life and living organisms. But Sibelius, moving on from the broad principles enunciated by Borodin, gave the process a new and more potent force through a profound intellectual power and a structural capacity a good way beyond and superior to Borodin's.

Nor does Sibelius's method equate with the use of the germ cell in the Beethoven sense; that again is something different. Beethoven was certainly an "organic" composer, the most comprehensive one yet known; but he worked, as he had to in his time, from different, less advanced evolutionary principles. All the same, in certain late works—the Grosse Fuge for example—that concentration of form and thought and interlocking of thematic motifs so typical of Sibelius in his maturity is not so much foreshadowed as already promulgated, if in a somewhat different manner. The germ cell and the source motif also appear in Sibelius; but again, neither is quite the same thing as the true nuclear structuring that is Sibelius's particular contribution to symphonic development. Beethoven would certainly have understood it and how it came about, even if he lived too early to have been able to go far along that specific line himself.

The opening of Sibelius's Second Symphony suggests that its model, if any, is going to be Brahms's Second, also in D. Both open with a rhythmic/thematic motif in the lower strings which contains germinal matter. The ensuing melodic evolutions are by no means alike, yet the overall similarities are obvious. On the other hand, the real significance lies deeper. The rising figure

which is embedded in the repeated notes of the opening bars of the Sibelius generates much of the subsequent material, not only in the first movement but throughout the symphony, either directly or in inversion. In the Brahms the initial motif is immediately spelt out and also acts as a kind of germcell for the whole symphony.

This outward correspondence between Sibelius and Brahms is on the face of it purely coincidental. Yet at another and more searching level, unconscious no doubt, it tells us a good deal more about the spontaneous receptivity of Sibelius's creative mind and its links with the broader stream of central European music. Indeed, superficially unlikely though the relationship may seem, Sibelius's first two symphonies parallel the first two of Brahms in several respects. In each case, the fundamental tone of the first is tragic and elegiac with a big tune in the finale, the second by contrast more lyrical and containing pastoral elements.*

In the D major Symphony it only takes a couple of bars to become clear that Sibelius and Brahms are set upon different courses, technically and structurally. This is inevitable: they were different men in different times.

The structure of the first movement in particular of the D major Symphony has caused some perplexity. The highly individual, typically Sibelian procedures led early commentators like Cecil Gray to speak of it as "a veritable revolution"† which introduces "an entirely new principle into symphonic form." Later critics have expended time and ingenuity trying to redress that somewhat exaggerated view by referring it back to some textbook idea of sonata form, much as certain critics, desperate for familiar signposts, have attempted to square the free forms of Beethoven's last sonatas and quartets with the same source. In the case of Sibelius, Gray was probably nearer the truth, though he overshot it, because at least he was aware of something unusual and genuinely creative about it.

The D major Symphony seems, superficially, to be an expansive work. Yet in its best parts it demonstrates that concentration of material and structure which is the essence of true symphonic form, and also of a genuinely twentieth-century aspect of thought and feeling. The finale is a fine paean of praise and strength, a sturdy affirmation of life and vitality in a broadly sweeping melodic expansion generated in the earlier movements. The force of nature is given full rein. The winds howl and roar; the tuba emits prodigies of elemental energy; strings scurry and swirl; and once again the great ostinato pedal points in the orchestra hold the foundations firm. Significantly, as in certain passages in the First Symphony, the melodic and harmonic structure veers noticeably toward modality. It is not yet an established principle; but its existence demonstrates that the strong

---

*These comparisons of Sibelius with other composers, Brahms, Borodin, Beethoven, Wagner, Elgar, whoever, are not to be taken as evidence of plagiarism or accusations of unwarranted eclecticism; but they may help redress a former imbalance whereby he was regarded as an isolated figure remote in his northern fastness, in the wrong and pejorative sense *original* (i. e. eccentric). In short they thrust him back into the European mainstream.

†*Sibelius* (Oxford University Press), p.35.

sense of modal polyphony in the later symphonies, especially the Sixth, was no unprecedented innovation but a logical consequence of ingredients already latent, and sometimes more than latent, from the outset.

Although the first movement of the Second Symphony is, like that of the First, the most original and positive in point of basic musical thinking and integration of material, it is dangerous to assume, as is often done, that the remaining three, in both cases, are comparatively regular and conventional. Whatever its lapses or shortcomings, any significant work of art, and orchestral symphony above all, has to be seen whole, taken as a complete realization of its original premises. If it can be dissected and its constituent parts isolated from the whole, it thereby implies a lack of that total integration upon which its specific assumptions depend. If the first movements of the First and Second symphonies of Sibelius appear upon initial analysis to be the most fruitful and genuinely creative, that is not only because of what they consist of in themselves, but no less because of what they subsequently give rise to. The highly individual and distinctive first movement of the Second Symphony passes through the sombre musings of the Andante with its brooding pizzicato basses and dramatic brass soundings and the bustling energy of the scherzo with its contrasting trio in a solitary folk mode, and finally opens out into the broad melodic expansion of the finale, its principle theme originating in the rising three notes of the symphony's opening bars. The comparative directness and simplicity of this melodic expansion, often thoughtlessly mistaken for a kind of naïve and unwarranted (in the contemporary context) optimism, is a direct outcome of the first movement's concentrated structure. This is not to say that there was no other possible outcome of the first movement's complex implications; but it was the one Sibelius chose.

The former patriotic associations of the D major Symphony, the finale a kind of sublimated *Finlandia* as protest against political oppression, have been dispelled by later research, notably in Tawastsjerna's exhaustive analysis. All the same, too much need not be read into that. The relationship between the conscious and the unconscious in the act of creation is total, not partial, that is, it applies to extramusical motivations as well as to the apparently coincidental interlinking of motifs and thematic resemblances. Thus when Tawaststjerna asserts that a theme in the finale was the result of the suicide of Sibelius's sister-in-law, Elli Järnefelt, it does not invalidate the general overall impression the symphony as a whole conveys, which is not bold and unashamed patriotic flag-waving, always a much too crude and simplistic interpretation.

Throughout the D major Symphony an exultant animism rides on the back of Sibelius's creative faculty. Yet the most truly Sibelian trait is the way in which the force and primeval vitalism is pitted against the intellectual integrity of the composer. No matter how daemonic the natural excesses may become, the mind of Sibelius has the measure of them. It is not overwhelmed, rendered impotent, reduced to chaos: it maintains its autonomy at all times. The story of how Sibelius wrote the slow movement in a hut on the snowline in the Italian Alps and how there came a ghostly knocking at the door, three times; how Sibelius went outside to investigate, but could find nothing, then went back to his score and immediately solved a problem that had been holding him up, is revealing. Sibelius was indestructible. There were no easy ways out.

At this stage Sibelius seems more or less content to give direct expression to the inherent forces in animate Nature. He is aware of natural hostility, but he does not, to any marked extent, come to grips with it. In a sense, he exults in the basic physical and impersonal natural daemonism and pandaemonism; he revels in it, takes it into his own consciousness and works his creative energies in harness with it, freely and without inhibition. It is here too that a more refined form of implied patriotism may be seen to operate. It is as though his feelings of exultance in natural force are linked with his pride of nation, landscape, and history. In the prevailing political situation, his mind would inevitably have been full of patriotic sentiments, sentiments that would have been transmuted into his work, not necessarily in the simplistic sense but as an underlying informing principle.

There is a sheer exuberance about the Second Symphony that stands in some contrast to the darker-hued, more tragic tones of the First, full of vital energy though that also is. But such an attitude to unregenerate nature could not indefinitely satisfy Sibelius. In the five years which separate the Second Symphony from the Third, he developed considerably, both in spiritual awareness and musical thinking. The natural daemonism of the Second is substantially absent from its successor, which has the outward appearance of a less portentous and less demanding product of Sibelius's genius.

This is true enough as far as it goes; but it is easy to miss the point of the apparent change or mellowing, a partial yielding of severity. The Third is the most immediately agreeable of Sibelius's symphonies; the least ominous and most genial. Parts of it are said to have been inspired by the fog banks which at certain times of the year move in ghostly procession along the southern English coasts. If this is in fact true, it puts the symphony into a new, for Sibelius, relationship with nature. The English climate, much less ferocious and menacing than the Finnish, may have inspired at least part of the geniality of the Third Symphony. At any rate, it was dedicated to Granville Bantock and has definite English associations, maybe in gratitude for the encouragement given to Sibelius's reputation, at the time of his first visit in 1905, by the English in general and Bantock in particular.

Between the Second and Third symphonies came the most explicitly programmed of his symphonic tone poems, *Pohjola's Daughter.* Like so much of Sibelius's music outside the symphonies, this was based upon an episode from the *Kalavela.* It tells how the magician-hero, ageing

Väinämöinen, homeward bound from military exploits in the North Lands (Pohjola), sees a beautiful maiden sitting on a rainbow spinning. The result is predictable. Overwhelmed by her radiant beauty he begs her to come down and join him; in the unchanging way of infinitely desireable women, the Maid of Pohjola returns him a crafty answer insisting that he prove his worth by accomplishing a series of impossible tasks, including building a boat out of the broken fragments of her spinning wheel. This proves quite beyond even his magical powers, so he is obliged to give up in despair, leaps back into his sleigh and continues his journey alone and greatly despondent. The score is prefaced by a substantial passage of verse adapted from the original source.

The music of *Pohjola's Daughter* follows the programme in some detail, unlike most of the other tone poems which evoke mood and atmosphere rather than essaying direct narrative. In this respect it stands nearest to Richard Strauss's *Till Eulenspiegel* or Elgar's *Falstaff* among other compositions of its period. All the same, the real significance of *Pohjola's Daughter* lies not in its narrative accuracy but in its musical structure and implication. The dark-hued opening cello motif not only provides the thematic genesis of the entire composition to which all else is related, it also establishes the unmistakable Sibelius tone that pervades all his music:

To quote on paper a Sibelius theme may encourage, to a greater or lesser extent, analysis of his music in terms of harmony, tonality, rhythmic impetus, or melodic cast, but his personal hallmark remains aural rather than visual; the key lies with the ear rather than the eye. No doubt this is true of any composer of strong individuality, but with Sibelius it is more true than with most.

Pohjola's Daughter confirms one important aspect of Sibelius's early creative evolution: he took a good deal longer to find his feet in symphony than in symphonic poem. This is only to be expected: symphony makes by far the greater demands. Neither of the first two symphonies suggest that the total realization of the artistic aim we find in the contemporary tone poems had been achieved; nor, though it represents a further important step along that difficult road, does the Third in all its parts. Both *The Swan of Tuonela* and *Pohjola's Daughter* achieve a unification of aim and realization, of form and content, of that is, ends and means, unmatched in the symphonies until the Fourth. And by then the innermost aesthetic and existential motivation had changed. No doubt at the time and in the context of Sibelius's contemporary development, the First and Second symphonies achieved all that could reasonably be required of them; but in the longer perspective they contain elements of Sibelius's journeywork and conventionalism alongside expressions of genuine and unmatchable Sibelian authenticity.

The opening of *Pohjola's Daughter* has a direct relationship to the opening of both the Third and Fourth symphonies, from opposing viewpoints, and not only because all three begin in the lower strings. The interlocking of aesthetic elements in different Sibelius compositions at a particular time are as notable as the interlocking of themes and motifs within a particular composition. In short, Sibelius's composing methods and his "tone of voice" are all of a piece. He did not adopt different, and often disparate methods and tone for different types of work. This does not mean that the tone and methods cannot be adapted to different tasks, with different requirements; simply that whatever he did, he remained uncompromisingly himself, through and through.

The English associations, such as they may have been, of the Third Symphony are revealing because they add a further dimension to our understanding of Sibelius's view of nature and his creative responses to it. Too much must not be read into these exterior factors, in this or any other work; but the clear lack of threatening gesture in the C major Symphony added to the probable impact of the English association, suggests a possible climatic relevance. And this is by no means uncommon in Sibelius. *Tapiola* could hardly have arisen out of an English winter landscape, however temporarily and incidentally severe.

But the real significance of the Third Symphony lies less in its content than in its structure. It has been (and still is) described as the most classical of all Sibelius's symphonies—whatever that in the particular context of the musical and social context of the 1900s may mean. Its first movement is taken as in the nearest to strict sonata form Sibelius ever produced; and in so far as that is true it constitutes its weakness, for, as Tovey rightly pointed out, Sibelius achieved his most memorable results precisely because his emancipation from the misconceived survival of sonata form is complete.

Yet the Third Symphony is by no means a reversion to an earlier style, his own or anyone else's, any more than the Fourth Symphony of Beethoven was a reversion to the style of Haydn or Mozart. The Beethoven Fourth is still often undervalued and misjudged because it appears to be smaller and more easy-going than its companions. It is as much *echt* Beethoven as any of the nine; and if the Sibelius Third is not upon that plane, it is still very much *echt* Sibelius and an important step towards his later masterpieces. For one thing, it marks a beginning of that paring down of symphonic form that is to play a leading part in the subsequent symphonies, sometimes to the point of enigma. By contrast with the first two symphonies, the Third asks for comparatively modest forces and shows a corresponding refinement of the former exuberance and excess. The scoring relies more than usual with Sibelius on the strings*; the former outbursts of brass and ominous invocations of woodwind are deliberately curbed. The menacing forest gods are for the time being mollified, black ice and gaunt granite crags temporarily foresworn. They will come back, all of them, and more; but here and now the sun shines more or less limpidly from behind breaks in the shifting fog banks.

The opening is musically and emotionally neutral, or nonaligned, one might say, in the sense that until the movement has evolved some way it is difficult to say what the exact initial premises are. If the opening of the Second Symphony suggests Brahms as a preliminary signpost, the opening of the Third is clearly related to the Second (B minor) Symphony of Borodin. The working out does not resemble the Borodin much more than the working out of the other follows Brahms; but there is the same energetic motif for lower strings, a similar rhythmic impetus, a matching gathering of strength through accumulation in strong forward motion. Sibelius begins

---

*Perhaps because of his early ambitions, never entirely crushed, to become a concert violinist, Sibelius always wrote particularly well for strings. But his scoring all through is remarkably distinctive and relevant to his orchestral thinking. He considered Mozart and Mendelssohn to have been the greatest masters of the orchestra, meaning thereby that when writing for the orchestra they, unlike masters of the piano, conceived it as a whole and thought clearly in terms of orchestral texture. He once declared that the great difference between the orchestra and the piano is that the former has no sustaining pedal, hence the frequency of those long pedal points in nearly all his orchestral scores. One wonders, however, if that goes far enough. Although he wrote only two small pieces for organ, the overall impression of his scoring and his treatment of the orchestra have, in a certain kind of homogeneity, relevance to the historic organ aesthetic. It has to be remembered that prior to the evolution of the modern symphony orchestra, the organ was the most powerful and most varied instrumental resource available to a composer. Modern organists tend to take heed of modern orchestral and chamber music techniques to expand and clarify the varieties of their registrations and so free themselves from the old charges of thickness and stolidity, of that is a certain lack of imaginative resource in respect of the potentialities of their instrument. The enlargement of resources expands both ways, and one wonders if this process may work also in reverse. Leopold Stokowski made a fascinating recording of the Sibelius Second Symphony in the late 1950s, which has newly been released on dell'Arte DA 9004. Stokowski began his career as an organist. Did his highly individual sense of orchestral blend and colour, here and elsewhere, derive in part from a profound understanding of organ technique and aesthetics in a contemporary context? The question probably cannot be answered; but it is worth asking.

Rosa Newmarch (Courtesy Music Information Centre, Helsinki)

Sibelius conducting the first performance of his Fifth Symphony in 1915 (Courtesy Music Information Centre, Helsinki)

Sibelius (Courtesy Music Information Centre, Helsinki)

Sibelius at work (Courtesy Music Information Centre, Helsinki)

and Borodin:

Yet straightforward and unaffected though Sibelius's opening is, it is one of the most difficult of all his first movements to "pace" satisfactorily, just as the middle movement is no less difficult to judge, though for different reasons.* Unlike most of Sibelius's melodies, this one is symmetrical, almost square cut. Yet the movement as a whole shows many true Sibelian features, not least in that motivic unity towards which all his symphony movements progress, and the "shunting" of form which was to lead eventually to the single movement of the Seventh Symphony. There is also more than a hint, darkening the otherwise luminous nature of the tonality, of the tritone which had appeared briefly in earlier Sibelius work and was to dominate the succeeding symphony, just as the modality which will infuse the Sixth is more than hinted at in the Third's middle movement.

The internal momentum of the opening theme soon propels another

as though out of itself, though in fact this has not only its distinctive existence but also generates in one of its phrases a typically Sibelian ostinato. The further working out shows Sibelius at his most subtle and inventive if not at his most imperative: he reserved that for the complex last movement, in pursuance it may have been of the post-Beethoven

*Robert Kajanus's historic 1932 recording with the London Symphony Orchestra, recently available from World Records, remains the only one to sound absolutely right in both sections. The pacing of both is convincing in a way no others are. In general, those conductors, like Bernstein, who get the first movement right miss the elusive quality of the second, usually by over-emphasis and too fast a tempo; while Barbirolli and Gibson who are good in the Andantino tend to make the first movement sound dull and aimless, largely through missing the underlying if undemonstrative athleticism. In both cases, of course, the failure comes from a lack of proper understanding of the true melodic structure. Anthony Collins, surprisingly, rushed both: Colin Davis comes nearest to Kajanus in total understanding. Oddly, although the finale is the most complex movement, more conductors handle it successfully than the other two—but perhaps it is not so odd: apparent simplicity is always deceptive.

tendency in symphonic writing to transfer the weight of the argument
from the first movement to the finale; at least to even the balance.

Indeed, it is precisely in this integration of movements, both thematically and formally through that "inner connection between all the
motives" which, for Sibelius, constituted the essence of the true symphonic style. Taking a lead out of certain of Beethoven's mid-period piano
sonatas and string quartets, Sibelius gives his second and third movement
in the C major Symphony what may best be called bifunctional forms. The
middle one, on the surface a predominantly gentle Andantino con moto,
quasi allegretto, incorporates elements of both true andante and potential
scherzando; while the finale combines the functions of scherzo and finale
proper. Formally, though not thematically, the first movement is as
self-contained as any normal symphonic movement; but from the opening
of the middle movement onwards there takes place a process of what can be
described as "squeezing". This occurs gently at first, then gradually
becomes firmer and stronger, until the latter part of the finale begins to
suggest a broad melodic expansion as in the Second Symphony but without
actually achieving it. The scherzando-scherzo formation of the latter part
of the middle movement and the first part of the third thus becomes a kind
of mobile energizing force between the beginning of the symphony and its
end. The Andantino itself, with its gently rocking motion between 6/4
and 3/2 and the constant shifting of accents is the most elusive of all
Sibelius's symphony movements (and with the first movement the most
difficult to bring off in performance): the flowing woodwind thirds and
quiet persistence of pizzicato strings seem frequently about to dissolve but
never actually do. Just as the conventional "big tune" never quite material-
izes at the end of the finale, so the dissolution of the Andantino is more
apparent than real. Like a good deal of Sibelius's music, though against the
run of the idea of him as little more than a crude and loudmouthed
provincial barker, the Third is in many aspects of itself a symphony of hints
and suggestions rather than of direct statement and display, in this respect
also containing embryonic anticipations of the Sixth.

Though the subtle motivic relationships in both the first movement
and the Andantino are entirely characteristic of Sibelius's symphonic style
and reveal a significant maturing of it, the highly organized scherzo-cum-
finale structure of the third movement is unquestionably the most complex
and most original part of the Third Symphony. Beginning with an
incipient 6/8 scherzo and moving later into an apparently straight 4/4
finale, it represents some further exploration of that thematic nuclear
construction of the first movement of the Second. Instead of direct thematic statement subsequently developed then recapitulated, splinters and
chips of theme are bandied about through the orchestra, apparently
unconnected but by the end clearly no such thing. The effect is cumulative, and if the expectation of a final emergence of full-blooded melody is
ultimately disappointed, so much has happened along the way that it

hardly seems relevant. The ambiguities are in the end more conclusive than any straight-on-the-table conclusion could have been in the context of the symphony as a whole. For the Andantino, Sibelius moved into the "remote" key of G-sharp minor; for the finale he returns to C major-A minor. This has the appearance of straightforward classical procedure. But in effect it is nothing of the sort: it bears no relation to Beethoven's way of clinching an argument, however arduous and complex along the way, by returning at the end to home ground, as in the C minor-C major juxtaposition of the Fifth Symphony or the more extended and comprehensive evolution from indecision in F major to ultimate triumph in C major in the squence of the three *Rasoumovsky* quartets. In the classical aesthetic the conclusion is invariably firm and direct, unambiguous; with Sibelius the enigma remains.

Although the first movement of the Sibelius Third Symphony can be analysed in terms of so-called sonata form, though it does not help much, the last movement cannot, even if for a passing convenience attempts have been, and still are, made. It is best, here as elsewhere, to recognize that the basic material always generates the form, not the other way round, and that to try to reduce the forms of works of art to preconceived notions is seldom helpful and usually misleading.

The Third Symphony meant much to Sibelius himself: he liked to say of it that it was "the most beloved and least fortunate of my children." It means no less to those who would understand the true inner meaning of his art and craft, comprehensively considered.

One of the leading characteristics of Sibelius's compositional methods is his frequent use of reiterated rhythmic patterns in ostinato. An example occurs in the finale of the Third Symphony, in trochaic metre. This is a device he used with remarkable effect in the tone poem *Nightride and Sunrise,* written around the same time. Unlike *Pohjola's Daughter,* there is no explicit programme. All the same, the provenance can hardly be mistaken, either from the title or from the music itself, at least the first part, the "nightride," just as there is no mistaking that of *Lemminkäinen's Return.*

The "ride" sets off at a great pace, not a hand gallop but a hell-for-leather rush through a landscape hedged with terror and dark forces, the pounding of horse's hooves invoked by an insistent trochaic metre* thematically deployed:

(See over)

---

*Trochaic meter—i.e. made up of units of trochees, in English prosody a metrical foot of two syllables, the first accented, the second unaccented, as − u / − u / − u / − u

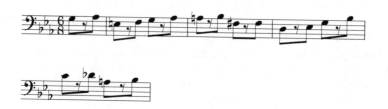

Not only the metric pattern but the harmonic structure also relates to the finale of the Third Symphony, and as often happens in a certain type of Sibelius composition, the terse rhythmic/thematic reiterations throw up a more sustained melodic idea:

This slowly begins to gain the ascendancy; but the trochees still persist for some time behind and underneath. (Is it stretching fancy too far to see, consciously or unconsciously in this galloping first section of *Nightride and Sunrise*—as well as in *Lemminkäinen's Return*—a distant legacy of Schubert's song *Der Erlkönig*; or still farther back and less ominously, the finale of Beethoven's piano sonata in D minor Op.31 No.2?)

The transition to "sunrise" is masterly. The metric foundation shifts from trochaic to even semiquavers (not for the first time but now decisively,) strings take over while little suggestive figures appear in the woodwind, and slowly the sun comes up in a resplendent glow of brass tone and a hinted foretaste of the end of the Fifth Symphony. Wagner spoke of music as "the art of transition," and Sibelius, both in his symphonies and his tone poems, shows a command of it rare in composers of his period and generation. Sibelius's compositions are anything but episodic; those of most of the romantic and postromantic symphonists tend to be precisely that, thus revealing a fundamental lack of true organic musical thinking.

No doubt sunrise in the far northern regions is not the same as sunrise on the European mainland; yet although the aims and methods are different, *Nightride and Sunrise* reveals, in reverse, a clear relationship with Wagner's evocation of "Dawn and Siegfried's Rhine Journey" in *Götterdämmerung*. The association, loose though it is, demonstrates once again both the receptivity and the independence of Sibelius's musical faculty, characteristics which will be further, and conclusively exposed in the next stage of his creative evolution.

2 : The Fourth Symphony -
The Pivot

The Third Symphony marks an important step forward in Sibelius's development. The brisk energy and clarity of its apparently unproblematic opening, and the general lack of violent gestures throughout have led to its being frequently rejected from the true Sibelius canon. Yet it was necessary for Sibelius to work his way through the technical revaluations of the Third before he could reach the masterpiece that is the Fourth. If the Third Symphony is, though often elusive and ambiguous, the most overall human of Sibelius's symphonies, its successor concentrates the Sibelian ethic and aesthetic with the utmost severity and austerity. And yet musically the Fourth derives several distinct elements from its under-valued predecessor, in certain aspects via the first two symphonies. There is no telescoping of individual movements, as in the Third; not even a running of two movements together as in the continuation of the scherzo into the finale of the Second. The Fourth Symphony has four clearly defined and separate movements; yet each is absolutely relevant to the whole by both internal and external reference. Indeed, not even in the Seventh, where symphonic form is finally distilled into a single continuous organism, is the motivic unity more total and all-pervading. The entire symphony is based upon the interval of an augmented fourth/diminished fifth, the tritone, immediately exposed in the germinating phrase of the first bar, muted lower strings and bassoon:

Subsequently, the tritone dominates each movement in one form or another, with the most ominous implication, undermining tonality and spiritual equilibrium alike, causing far-reaching musical and metaphysical effects. Though the Fourth Symphony is nominally in A minor the insistence of the tritone prevents the emergence of any clear tonality; even the third movement (in effect the slow movement, if the first had not also answered that description, being marked quasi adagio) which relies upon the interval of a fifth, seems to wander fatalistically as though awaiting the visitation. And the finale, brisk and at first apparently breezy though it is, soon begins to disintegrate, again under threat of the tritone which now reestablishes its predominance, and ends in a croak of desolation.

In most artists' catalogues there is a key work, one which enshrines all the leading characteristics of style and technique and so becomes, both forwards and backwards, the kernel of the entire nut. It may not necessarily be the best or greatest, considered overall, though it frequently is; but it remains central; a summation if not inevitably a consummation. Henry James used to say that embedded in all his novels was a single sentence or passage that provided the key to the whole, and that once the reader had discovered and recognized it the overall meaning of the story became clear.* The existence of a key, or pivot work in a composer's or writer's total production is not exactly analagous; but its function can be seen to be very much the same in the larger context.

In the case of Sibelius there is little doubt that the Fourth Symphony fulfills that particular role (as well as several others): once the listener has come to terms with the Fourth Symphony, come to a proper understanding of it, made it his or her own, as again Henry James would say, the total art of Sibelius falls into place.

The thematic and harmonic outlines of the Fourth Symphony are cryptic and enigmatic beyond anything even Sibelius himself had achieved before; symphonic form is pared to the bone; and even where extended melody is suggested expectation is not only unfulfilled, but hardly predicted. Throughout, Sibelius composes from the basic elements of music; nuclei of melody, harmony, and rhythm interweave and interlock as he contemplates the elements of organic life, in and out of nature. The tonal foundations remain ambiguous, even apart from the activities of the

*The most famous instance is that of *The Ambassadors* and the sentence about "living all you can".

tritone. In many places Sibelius more than hints at both atonality and polytonality without actually breeching either directly.

The Fourth Symphony is frequently remarked on, and usually praised, for its economy. This is perfectly justified: it is probably the most economical composition of its kind ever written. To praise a work of art for its economy is meaningless unless economy is inherent in its creative postulates, just as it is irrelevant to condemn another for opulence or luxury when opulence and luxuriance are clearly constituent parts of its inner nature—an economical Wagner would be as great an aberration as a profligate Webern. Sibelius himself moved from the comparative opulence of the First Symphony through the restraints of the Third to the stringent economy of the Fourth. Having worked through the wide gamut from the one to the other, he was subsequently free to employ elements of each as he pleased and as his creative impetus required. This is another aspect of the Fourth Symphony that makes it the vital pivot work in Sibelius's catalogue.

Sibelius himself in a letter to Rosa Newmarch, wrote that the Fourth Symphony was "a protest against the compositions of today," with "absolutely nothing of the circus about it." In this he partly deceived himself; or at least mistook the precise meaning of what he was saying. Certainly, there is "nothing of the circus" about the Fourth Symphony; and no less certainly it runs strongly against the grain of many contemporary compositions—but that is not the whole story.

Let us consider: the musical world of the period at the inception and completion of the Fourth Symphony, roughly between 1909 and 1911, a world with the grandiose conceptions of Mahler, the opulences of Richard Strauss. Mahler's Ninth Symphony appeared in 1909. All Strauss's major tone poems with the exception of the *Alpine Symphony* had been completed, as well as *Salome* and *Elektra,* and he was about to turn his back on the future with the disarming pastiche of *Der Rosenkavalier,* a work of undoubted genius and absolute allure, but hardly facing up to the contemporary *Zeitgeist.* Schoenberg was still in the process of leaving behind him the post-*Tristan* chromaticisms of *Verklaerte Nacht, Pelleas und Melisande* and *Gurrelieder.* Stravinsky was beginning to find his way with *The Firebird* and *Petrushka,* the famous riot of *The Rite of Spring* still ahead by at least two years. Debussy's late masterpieces were still to come or had only just appeared in the case of the orchestral *Images.* On the surface it looked as though the musical scene contained all the ingredients of a circus.

In a letter of 1913 to Rosa Newmarch, Sibelius allowed himself some sarcasm at the expense of composers, who "are still writing in the post-Wagnerian style—with the same laughable pose and the still more laughable would-be profundity." The guilty parties could easily be identified, and for the most part deserved the censure. Some, like Delius, retreated into a private dreamworld of great beauty and haunting nostalgia which, however tough and hard-fibred the mind that produced it, was still a passionate regret for lost Edens of the soul. Others, like Scriabin, took off in an intoxication of mysticism from which there was no possible return to reality.

But there remained the other side of the picture, and in the end the one which mattered. Schoenberg had already produced the epitome of concision in the Three Little Orchestral Pieces (1910) and the Piano Pieces Op. 11 (1908) and Op. 19 (1911). Webern was writing some of his most intense orchestral and chamber works, all of them remarkable for a brevity in line with Schoenberg's Three Little Pieces, and even more remarkable for their surcharged concentration. And from the point of view of formal integration, Schoenberg had already gone some way towards total fusion of movements in the First String Quartet (1905) and the First Chamber Symphony (1906). In France too the reaction had already set in. When the poet Paul Verlaine raised the cry "ring the neck of rhetoric," the musicians such as Fauré and Ravel echoed it in their essentially civilized, elegant, sophisticated Gallic compositions, a turning of the back on extravagance and overblown luxuriance of both form and content.

Thus from one point of view Sibelius, far from issuing a "protest against the compositions of today," was simply moving in accord with the important aesthetic evolutions of the period. It is true that the textural as well as the formal and intellectual severity of the Fourth Symphony give it a penny plain appearance even outside the realms of post-Wagnerian opulence. On the other hand, all post-Wagnerian composition was in essence backward-looking, dusk rather than dawn, the sunset glow instead of a new sunrise, however hesitant and initially flawed, ringed by cloud and the mists of indecision.

For Sibelius there was no indecision. He had worked his passage to and through the Fourth Symphony some way in advance of many who came out of the nineteenth century and were still floundering in the shallows as its tides receded. The Fourth Symphony of Sibelius is essentially prophetic, not in the superficial sense of predicting events and consequences to come but in the Walt Whitman sense of revealing the indwelling source and principle of life—in this case the source and principle of life in the twentieth century—the sense in which all true art is prophetic.

The later fashion for economy and concision came on the physical side in the wake of the holocaust of the First World War, which not only brought a kind of human conceit down from its former empyrean heights, but also left a trail of despoliation and impoverishment more than material. But in fact long before that, almost before the turn of the century, a change had begun to take place in the European psyche, as though in unconscious recognition of nemesis to come if the old attitudes and assumptions were not drastically modified. The sense of optimism, born of the Age of Enlightenment and fostered by the idea of the inevitability of progress began to break up under the stress of scientific research, and the resulting uncertainty over man's destiny. With the early twentieth century came the realization that instead of the rainbow at the end of the road, there was something very different, perhaps as yet not clearly definable, but without doubt thoroughly disquieting. It may have been a healthier view, a lifting of the veil, clearing of the vision; but it still came as something of a shock to those basking in an old dream or lamenting some lost paradise that had gone forever, or more likely never was. Freud and the unconscious; Einstein and Rutherford and the splitting of the atom: suddenly the potentialities seemed unlimited; but so did the dangers. The human mind and spirit were in a new kind of peril, alienated in a hostile environment. In some ways it was a return to the condition of primitive man, who was also cast loose in a hostile environment. But now there was a difference: man had knowledge, and with knowledge a sophistication of technique. But all the time the forces of violence and destruction were gaining force and strength, in certain ways precisely because of that acquired knowledge.

The warning note had to be sounded. And one of the most imperative was sounded by Sibelius, especially in the Fourth Symphony. Partly because he lived and worked at a climatic as well as a geographical remove from the centre of European civilization, partly because of an inborn bias of temperament, (and the two are, of course, connected) Sibelius was able to formulate certain psychic conditions from a different angle; and being a true creative artist, he formulated also a new aspect of technique to expound them. Thomas Mann spoke in *Doktor Faustus,* of a dark deposit of myth and saga in the German soul. One aspect of this came to the surface in Wagner; another side in Hitler and the Nazis.* The same is true of Finland and the Northlands in general, where this deposit lies still nearer the surface and in an even purer form. Indeed, Wagner's mythology was derived from Norse sources and then infected with the virus of nineteenth-century High Romanticism. Sibelius's close physical proximity to and imaginative identification with the Finnish mythology gave him a particular psychological bias probably impossible for a composer or poet from the Catholic Latin south, or even from the more fluid European centre. In this respect, Sibelius with his penetration of both ancient saga and contemporary sophisticated civilization, forms a link between the two aspects of man isolated and at peril in a hostile natural environment, at a distance of countless centuries in time, and across a far larger gap of psychological and imaginative time. The Fourth Symphony has, like any important work of art, various aspects; but one of these is an imaginative distillation of the dilemma of man confronted by the two opposite poles of his evolutionary consciousness. The Fourth

---

*The relationship between Wagner and the Nazis—that is, between the high peak of Romanticism and the ultimate romantic decadence—is still in need of clarification. It is close, but not in the way it is too easily and too conveniently assumed to be.

Symphony is both a warning and a premonition*

The extreme economy of the Fourth Symphony in a musical context recalls—or by implication anticipates—Ernest Hemingway's argument that a writer can leave out anything he wants to so long as he knows it, but if he leaves out what he does not know, the reader will see through him and the story will be a fake. †

One of Hemingway's main achievements was to bring the novel and short story out of the discursive nineteenth century into the harder-edged, less expansive twentieth. Sibelius, twenty years earlier, had begun to do almost exactly the same thing with the full-scale orchestral symphony and symphonic poem. ‡ The Fourth is the apogee of that process—further reduction of symphonic style and structure was impossible without the kind of emaciation that would have destroyed it altogether, just as further reduction of Hemingway's finest prose would destroy it no less. Sibelius and Hemingway have a number of stylistic devices in common. I have already drawn attention to Sibelius's ability to produce both long, flowing, asymmetrical melodies as well as short, terse, energizing thematic nuclei. In the same way, much of the effect of Hemingway's prose derives from the way he frequently contrasts the familiar "tough", cryptic sentences with long, sinewy, malleable ones. Without that particular juxtaposition, especially in the full length novels and books, the effect would be only of a kind of repetitous monotony, a machine-gun stuttering without the flexibility to express the necessary range of mood and emotion or the adaptability to create character.

Thus total mastery, for writer and composer, lies in the knowledge, both instinctive and acquired through experience, of when to expand and when to contract. If Sibelius in his later symphonies, notably the Fourth and Sixth (but not only in the symphonies), appears often to leave out more than he puts in, especially in the matter of extended melody, it is not because he does not know about melody (he had already demonstrated that

---

*It is necessary again to insist upon the relationship between the conscious and the unconscious in both the conception and the appreciation of works of art. The distinctive musical language of the Fourth Symphony can be studied and analysed, and valid interpretations deduced. But the deeper implications lie behind the language, not directly in what is said but still more in what is left out.

†Hemingway liked to say of one of his best know stories, *The Killers,* that he had "left out the whole city of Chicago." (See A. E. Hotchner's *Papa Hemingway,* Mayflower Books, p. 141. See also *Death in the Afternoon,* p. 183, for more general remarks on putting in and leaving out.) Dramatizers and film makers have an incurable habit of putting back what the author has deliberately left out. With composers it is somewhat different. Although musical compositions are by no mean immune from the attentions of cutters and carvers, no one has yet found a way of putting back into a musical composition what the composer in his judgment has left out.

‡This of course relates to Sibelius's disagreement with Mahler over the true nature of the symphony. Sibelius pushed the symphony in the opposite direction to Mahler, arriving ultimately, via the Fourth and Sixth, at the final synthesis of the Seventh. But just as Hemingway applied the same principles to the short story, so Sibelius did the same with symphonic poem and other related compositions, moving always in the direction of greater unity and concision and away from discursivess and the picturesque.

in the First and Second symphonies and other contemporary compositions), but because the particular cast of his musical thinking and the
functioning of his creative faculty at that specific time and in that context
required it. It is in this sense that works like the Fourth and Sixth
symphonies, *The Bard,* even the delightful *Rakastava,* seem so highly
charged, sound always as though they contain immense internal signfi-
cances that are suggested rather than delivered. Even in the Fourth
Symphony, where the melodic paragraphs are ruthlessly and deliberately
curtailed, the associated tonal and harmonic structure stripped bare, the
first part of the finale appears to be on the point of releasing melodic and
impulsive generosities, as though the principle of laying longer, more
pliable sentences alongside the concentrated thematic nuclei is about to be
honoured. But it does not come out like that: before long an unnerving
process of disintegration begins which by the end has become total and
irreconcilable. The last pages die away into a kind of resigned nothingness,
with a thrice repeated figure from a solo oboe as of some mythical creature
uttering a cry of infinite loneliness in the frozen wastes of the spirit, or
perhaps an invocation of infinite pain in infinite desolation—the human
spirit at last in total alienation from a bleak, bitter, and everlastingly
hostile environment.

If the opening of the Second Symphony very loosely suggested
Brahms, and the opening of the Third an aspect of Borodin, the Fourth
Symphony, beginning to end, sounds like nothing but the quintessence of
Sibelius. The first movement, tempo molto moderato, quasi adagio, lasts
only 114 bars but is so concentrated and "dense" that most symphonists
between Beethoven and Sibelius would have made half a dozen mountains
out of its basic material. The tritone dominates, not only in the opening
phrase but throughout. No other hundred odd bars of symphonic music
have such an extraordinary specific gravity. Individual themes are virtually
impossible to separate from the continuously evolving texture: organic
musical thinking preludes conventional analytical division and separation.

The second movement, Allegro molto vivace, is a scherzo by repute
rather than by nature. It begins with a piece of melody for the oboe, which
may sound pastoral by association but little else:

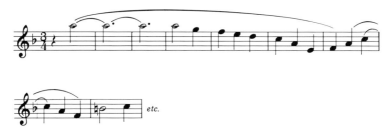

The augmented fourth comes in a rising two-note figure

also on the oboe. An initial retrospect might suggest that it promotes, in inversion, the oboe croak of the last page—until it is recalled that the figure itself appears in combination with the other.

Eighteen bars later (and in this context eighteen bars is a long stretch), at B in the score, the time changes from 3/4 to 2/4 and a curiously offhand theme appears in unison strings, with another insistent rhythm:

These motifs are allowed to grow and inject insidious cross references through into what work-a-day criticism likes to call the "trio." Then, as if about to begin all over again, Sibelius snaps the entire movement off short with a shrug of the shoulders and three taps on the drum.*

The third movement is sometimes described as "rhapsodic"—which may usually be taken as an admission that its form is even more enigmatic than the others. It begins with a motif for two flutes:

This moves uncertainly in the woodwind, supported by subdued strings, which introduce, in the cellos, a small pivotal figure, bred out of Ex.5; this gives

---

*This is simply an extension of the way Beethoven ends the scherzi of the Seventh and Ninth symphonies.

which then grows into what purports to be the main theme

which as the movement evolves tries twice to achieve the status of a fully fashioned melody, but backs off each time, first when disuaded by the return of the opening motif, secondly when crushed by the brass.

The entire movement is built out of these two motifs. But this in itself does not mean very much. It depends on the use of those motifs; whether they are made part of a process of continuous organic growth, or simply bandied about in a fanciful and entertaining manner, stood on their heads, turned inside out, set to chasing each other by the tail. The latter may produce excellent and skillfully wrought music, but it is not symphonic thinking. It is the primary distinction of Sibelius's use of motifs and themes that it is genuinely organic, an inner evolutionary process that constitutes the principle of true growth, rather than simple accumulation or complex mathematical combination. *

The finale sets off with a theme on the strings that bears an internal (internal within this particular symphony, that is) relationship to the opening oboe theme of the scherzo. It has a generous curve and a fine propulsive energy. This gives way to a motif first given by a solo cello which in its turn relates to the string motif in the scherzo (Ex.4). The movement is helped on its exhilaratingly frosty way by a number of "whoops" on wind and strings, and further characterized by the inclusion of *Glocken* ("bells"–not Glockenspiel, which is different).

The other significant motif is a chorale-like theme, very Sibelian in its tone and contour:

(See over)

---

*The principle of organic growth is not even outlined by a quotation of leading motifs: in it everything is an essential part of the whole and contributes directly to its inner energy.

So far so good. But it is not in the end good at all. The structure cracks, slips, calling briefly to mind Yeats's lines, "Things fall apart; the centre cannot hold . . ."

The structure of the Fourth Symphony as a whole makes a fascinating study in musical aesthetics. It further explores certain aspects of technique derived from Beethoven, notably the compression of form and the use of a kind of sketch treatment. But the most striking feature is the way in which Sibelius, while apparently adhering to the traditional four-movement symphonic form, in fact makes a number of significant moves towards total unification. The balance of movements is especially telling: if the second movement relates to the finale (see examples above), the first and third are no less internally connected. This, in both cases, goes far beyond the obvious relationships of tempi, though these too are important.

In some of his works Beethoven achieved, either by deliberate design or instinctively, a kind of overall structure in which four movements had the weight of three - the most familiar example is the Eighth Symphony. Here two small movements are placed between two large ones, so that the specific gravities come out as $1 = 1(2) = 1$, making not four but three. Although Beethoven produced the most convincing examples of this kind of thing, it was already inherent in the late classical sonata style. Brahms however, tended to push it too far, by making the two middle movements added together still too light for the outer ones.

Sibelius's way of fusing two or more movements together is no more than an extension and modification of the same basic principle. A necessary part of the continuing evolution of symphonic form and structure, it was the kind of evolution that most post-Beethoven symphonists either evaded or did not recognize.

Critics will argue that the Fourth Symphony, like the Sixth, has four clear and independent movements: neither has even the formal gesture of a link between two movements as in the Second where, following Beethoven, Sibelius runs scherzo into finale—though with a much simpler and less sophisticated handling of the transition.

True; but the argument is not invalidated by an apparent contradiction. In fact, the latent integration within the Fourth and Sixth symphonies goes so far that the complete formal integration of the Seventh is not only possible but inevitable. It is not simply a question of the pairing of the Fourth into 2 + 2; not even the persistence of the tritone in three of those movements and the threat of it in the third. It is a matter of the fundamental thought-process; the way in which despite the outer, physical divisions, the symphony emerges from the mind of its creator and enters that of the listener as a single, unified whole; the unconscious impression of total integration confirmed by precise knowledge of its total motivic unity. The same is true of the Sixth, though from a slightly different viewpoint.

Whether, and if so to what degree, the threat of death from throat cancer hangs over the Fourth Symphony is now difficult to determine, nor is it any longer all that important. Even if such a threat was initially responsible for setting the tone of the work, it would have acted only as a kind of trigger. The content of the Fourth Symphony is concerned with more than personal fears and depressions. It is usually regarded as an essentially tragic symphony, gloomy even. But it is probably more accurate to see it as the expression of a particular kind of tragic stoicism; of broken faith seeking its point of identification in a hostile universe. It is not dramatic tragedy, in the sense implied when Yeats heard Lady Gregory assert, as he wrote in *A General Introduction for My Work,* "Tragedy must be a joy to the man who dies." There is not much joy here, anywhere; and what hint there is of it at the beginning of the finale is soon extinguished. At bottom, the Fourth Symphony of Sibelius postulates a stoical acceptance of a tragic world- and life-view in the face of inimical nature; and it analyses the essence of those inimical forces with total integrity. Perhaps it is most truly seen in terms of the Hegelian tragedy of consciousness.

Returning to my earlier comparison between Sibelius and Hemingway, the description of the author at the Nobel Prize citation for literature in 1954, could also have been applied to the composer, "One of those who, honestly and undauntedly, reproduces the genuine features of the hard countenance of the age."*

In his post-romantic (i.e. post-*Tristan*) works, Schoenberg pushed chromaticism as far as it could go. In the Fourth Symphony Sibelius pushed the infrastructure of tonality as far as it would go in the opposite direction. And as so often happens, on the principle that apparent opposites always tend to complete the circle and meet at a common point, the upshot in the historical context was either actual or potential atonality. The implications were inescapable: Schoenberg accepted them unequivocally; Sibelius saw them as a kind of crisis of tonality itself. The difference, though of profound importance, tended to revolve around the same central pivot.†

---

*The difference of course lay in intellectual content. Hemingway's approach to life and fiction was basically one of gut reaction. Sibelius on the other hand revealed throughout his life a powerful intellect forming and shaping his compositions.

†Sibelius, like Mozart, is often referred to as a musical conservative. But the term is ambivalent.

Formally, though not tonally or harmonically, Sibelius and Schoenberg were running on roughly parallel courses. Nearly twenty years before Sibelius's Seventh Symphony, Schoenberg in his D minor String Quartet and First Chamber Symphony had already begun the process of fusing the separate movements of traditional sonata form into a single continuous whole. Though Schoenberg at this stage did not go as far as Sibelius in the Seventh—the ultimate in what is known as portmanteau form—and later followed a different direction, the contemporary evolution of musical form and aesthetics can hardly be mistaken. And although Sibelius did not go all the way to portmanteau form until the Seventh Symphony of 1924, the ultimate symphonic synthesis, all his symphonies and several of his symphonic poems from at least the Third onwards, are moving purposefully towards that consummation. At the same time, by again divergent methods, Webern was working towards an even more drastic concision and a more radical approach to form and technique. But the overall ambience remained; and Sibelius was a significant part of it. Indeed, in severity of musical thought and the uncompromising nature of his spiritual and aesthetic premises, the Sibelius of the Fourth Symphony was in advance of Schoenberg and on a par with Webern, certainly in the pre-First World War decade. And from his published statements—"a protest against the compositions of today" in respect of the Fourth Symphony, "pure cold water" of the Sixth—it is clear that Sibelius felt no compunction about what he was doing. He did not feel, as Schoenberg did, a fierce internal resistance to his own innovations, even though in the case of Sibelius the innovations were more directly evolutionary, less iconoclastic. Yet the Fourth Symphony of Sibelius was, in the context of its period and its stylistic postulates (the full-scale orchestral symphony), as radical and as perplexing to those who first heard it as the First Chamber Symphony of Schoenberg was in relation to its own contemporary situation. And the Sibelius, unlike the Schoenberg, was not even a transitional work but a logical culmination at that point in time, as well as a prophecy.

That the stylistic and aesthetic postulates of the Fourth Symphony were central to Sibelius's overall musical thinking and creative impulses at the time is shown by certain other works, very different in content but closely related in terms of style and technique, that lie adjacent to it. The most notable of these are the tone poem *The Bard* and the suite *Rakastava,* quite different in content but markedly similar in style. Also to this period

---

What is usually meant is that neither was an experimenter or innovator with musical language and vocabulary, but each was content to remain broadly within the bounds of established usage. This is both true and not true: true if it means a heightening and expansion of the fundamental principles of life and art; untrue if it implies a slavery to convention and working by precept. In any case, a determination to revolutionize language does not necessarily make a good revolutionary. Many who play fast and loose with language only end by proving that they have nothing to say. A concern with language for its own sake is often valuable, sometimes necessary. But it does not end there: the true meaning and significance of language lies beyond language itself.

belongs the "tone poem for soprano and orchestra", *Luonnotar,* one of the most purely beautiful and genuinely original compositions outside the symphonies. It is the most strikingly dramatic of all his vocal works, and the one which shows what he might have achieved if he had seriously turned his hand to opera or music drama.* These are three of Sibelius's most highly personal masterpieces on a smaller scale. Each one explores in a short space some aspect of his style that may easily be overlooked because there is little time or opportunity for it in the more familiar symphonic compositions. The same is true, though from yet another standpoint, of *The Oceanides,* which shares with *Tapiola* the circumstance of having been written to an American commission, and stands alone among Sibelius's important tone poems in having nothing to do with Finnish saga or mythology.

The Bard is probably the least appreciated of the tone poems. This is not surprising: most of the familiar Sibelius hallmarks are missing; nearly all the more subtle internal ones operative. There are no big gestures, as the title might suggest; no thumpings of the breast or raisings of the voice. Though scored for large orchestra, the resources are used sparingly and with almost wilfull restraint. Much imaginative use is made of the harp, which has unusual prominence. It is a piece which leaves a thoroughly ambiguous and enigmatic impression on the mind. It suggests a whole imaginative world that it never actually states or defines. It is a masterpiece of omission.

One cannot even begin to guess what is left out of *The Bard*—except that Sibelius himself knew it all. Hints and wisps of theme drift around through continually alternating time signatures—common, 3/4, 2/4, 4/4—with a typically Sibelian pervading motif:

Even the declamatory outburst does nothing to disturb the mood of introverted mystery. It is not even clear whether the basic tone is one of sadness, serenity, memory, or pride. Perhaps it is a mixture of all these and more.

Very different is *Rakastava* ("The Lover"). This is curious from several points of view. It began as a piece for *a cappella* male voice choir, in 1893, which Sibelius during the next five years rearranged first with string accompaniment, then for mixed chorus. Nobody knows just why Sibelius returned to it a dozen years later and transformed it into a suite for strings, timpani and triangle; and for a long time nobody was quite sure when, but it is now generally accepted that the transformation took place in or around

---

*See "Sibelius and the Theatre."

1911, the year when the Fourth Symphony appeared. And transformation is the right word. This is among the most beautiful, the most heart-warming, the most human of Sibelius's compositions. He who is still so often thought of as invariably remote, unapproachable, cold at heart, and unmotivated by any trace of real human emotion, here shows both his heart and his understanding of the heart; a subtle, generous, warm-blooded penetration of the emotions of love and the feelings of the lover. It is music of charm and delicacy, but also of true substance as it ranges from hope to joy and then reflects upon the sadness and transience of young love. It too is a masterpiece.

Both the melodic and the harmonic structure of *Rakastava*'s three movements are typical of the mature Sibelius at his most resourceful. Again, there are no big gestures, no rhetorical outbursts; yet the effect is quite different from *The Bard*. By this time Sibelius's technique had achieved great richness and flexibility. He was never perhaps a genuinely versatile composer—his basic manner was too personal, too distinctive, for that—but his style could be turned to a variety of tasks, both large and small while still retaining its independence. Always adept at writing for strings, Sibelius exhibits in *Rakastava* both the range and the subtlety of his skill, just as the melodic and harmonic content reveals the range and subtlety of his musical thinking. Attractive and melodious though it is, *Rakastava* is by no means the simple, straightforward "Love Song" suite it is occasionally assumed to be. Apart from the sadness of parting in the last movement, the harmonic and metric displacements, characteristic of Sibelius but used to unusual effect here, have the effect of the knife gently slipped between the ribs—the inevitable concomitant of all love not merely childish and sentimental. The lyricism is tinged.

The first movement is remarkable for the intensity of its melodic outlines and their harmonic and metric foundations: also for the wide spacing between the top line of the upper strings and the basses, another Sibelius trademark from the Fourth Symphony. The middle movement has a delicate grace and charm rare in Sibelius—and not only in Sibelius. Subtitled "The Way of the Lover," it has a lightness of step and a gaiety of heart perfectly suggested by the pliant main theme and the buoyancy of rhythm:

(See over)

The entry of pizzicato double basses, very quietly, at four after B causes one to catch the breath; and the ending, seemingly terse, almost abrupt, like a sudden quick wave of the hand, is in direct parallel to the ending of the Fourth Symphony's scherzo.*

---

*Rakastava is not an easy work to perform satisfactorily; and the middle movement in particular is seldom given the grace and buoyant delicacy it requires. It is often made to sound either too emotionally indulgent or too bland. The best of all recorded versions came on an old Russian MK

disc imported in the 1960s, by Rozhdestvensky and the Moscow Radio Symphony Orchestra, where this middle movement in particular was irresistable. The record (DO11339) also contained a remarkable version of the Seventh Symphony, marred only by a first trombone whose vibrato was so exaggerated it raised suspicions that someone had been at the vodka. A serious blot on a fine interpretation. The *Rakastava,* still sounding marvellously fresh and idiomatic, has reappeared on HMV Melodiya ASD3672, coupled with the First Symphony.

The third and last movement–"Goodnight, my love! Farewell!"–is the most complex and extended of the three. It opens with a theme given by a solo violin that is derived by a characteristically Sibelian process from a secondary motif in the first movement. Though *Rakastava* is not a symphony, or even a symphonic poem in the loosest sense, it too has its inner motivic unity, its interlocking of themes and motifs. The working out of this third section or movement, through several apparently independent sections is an example of simplicity through overt complexity (or complexity through simplicity). Its several sections are not, finally, unrelated but differing aspects of the same creative process. Like the whole of *Rakastava*, despite the superficial attractiveness and lyric charm, it confirms Blake's assertion that simplicity is not the same as insipidity. *Rakastava* is anything but insipid: it is one of Sibelius's most perfect and most revealing smaller scale compositions. It relates in its stylistic premises not only to the Fourth Symphony, but in its modal inflections and undemonstrative tone, it anticipates the Sixth. Thus it too is in its own way a pivot work, absolutely essential to a proper understanding of Sibelius's art considered as a whole.

So from another point of view is *The Oceanides,* a work that produces a totally different impression, and one again unique in Sibelius's output, and unusual in its non-Finnish, or Nordic, origins. It is based on Homer, the Oceanides being the nymphs that lived in the waters of classical antiquity. All his life Sibelius had a passion for Greek and Latin classical culture and art. It is not the mainspring of his own creative work, but it was an important part of his makeup as man and artist. It could be said of him, as of Nietzsche, that foremost in his life- and world-view was the Greek idea of the conquest of pessimism through art. This was to become more exteriorized as he grew older; but it is latent in his entire approach to life and art.

The Oceanides is thus sea, or water music, essentially. Perhaps in roughly contemporary compositions its nearest equivalent is Arnold Bax's *The Garden of Fand.* * *The Oceanides* is still often referred to as a rare example of Sibelius flirting with a kind of Debussyian "impressionistic" technique. This idea originated with the pioneer of Sibelius appreciation in England, the late Cecil Gray whose book, first published in 1931, influenced a whole generation of Sibelius critics and listeners, and maybe more than one generation. Gray even spoke of "pointillisme" in the scoring. Loosely, there may be something to be said for it; but it is a superficial judgment, based upon some external devices of orchestration. At the deeper and more meaningful level, the scoring of *The Oceanides* is by no means unique in Sibelius: it simply concentrates more than usual on certain aspects of his normal practice in earlier works. Like a number of other composers, Beethoven and Elgar among them in their concertos, Sibelius would sometimes concentrate on devices of scoring in tone poems, or suites of theatre music in a manner (experiments would be too strong a word) for which there was little scope in the more rigorous context of the symphonies. This is not of course to argue that the symphonies of Sibelius, any more than those of Beethoven and Elgar, are deficient in resourceful orchestration. With Sibelius in particular the scoring is an integral part of the musical thinking; but there is inevitably less opportunity to explore orchestral colour and manipulation for its own sake, so to say, in the overall context of symphonic evolution. In *The Oceanides* certain innate aspects of Sibelius's orchestral technique and method are deliberately pushed to their extremes.

Yet *The Oceanides* as a whole is as indelibly stamped with Sibelius's musical finger prints as any of his compositions. None but the composer of *Rakastava* or *The Bard* could have written the opening bars; no one but Sibelius could have handled woodwind and brass in quite the same way. The "pointilliste" argument gets nowhere: the blend and conjunction of orchestral colour is in no sense analogous with the technique of the pointilliste painters. Perhaps on paper the score does suggest some such immediate impression; but the ear soon corrects it. The use of harp harmonics, as in *The Bard,* can cause a superficial judgment to veer towards impressionism; and indeed, impression of a kind is certainly intimated. But *impressionism* in musical terms is a word loosely used and not at all precise in definition.

A number of lesser compositions for orchestra come from the years either side of the central Fourth Symphony. Both *The Dryad* (1910) and

---

*The Oceanides has no programme, unlike *The Garden of Fand* which has a detailed one.

Pan and Echo (1906) might seem from their titles to share with *The Oceanides* a Greek origin in Sibelius's mind, though there is no other intimation of it and in neither case does the music itself suggest as much. Both works, as well as the *Dance Intermezzo* (1907), may justly be described as "petit Sibelius," characteristic but without the inner motivation which distinguishes his finest work. The Funeral March, *In Memoriam,* produced in 1909 but conceived in embryo some years earlier, is a somewhat different case. A massive, sonorous piece, sombre in tone and with some dramatic gestures, it has taken a good deal of stick from some critics. It gives the impression of Sibelius consciously delivering himself of public rather than private utterance. * It has been compared, to its disadvantage, with the elegiac music of Beethoven, Wagner, and Chopin, none of which is directly relevant. Probably the best and worst that can be said about it is that, like all "public" music, it celebrates a general in place of a personal grief. Perhaps the closest anology, in mood but not in virtuosity or the technique of reminiscence, is with Tennyson's *Ode on the Death of the Duke of Wellington.* That is a masterpiece of public expression, of art rising to an occasion of national mourning which can hardly be said of *In Memoriam.* Yet the Sibelius has its own limited power and dignity, and a mature skill in execution.

Whichever way one looks at it, the Fourth Symphony appears as the pivotal work in Sibelius's catalogue. In Sibelius's created universe it occupies the place of a major planet surrounded by a number of satelites, some of them of exceptional quality.

---

*Some have suggested that it was inspired by a personal loss. Sibelius's eldest daughter said it was intended to commemorate the young Finnish patriot, Eugen Schauman, who assassinated a Tsarist senior official in 1904. Sibelius himself said that the idea for it first came to him in Berlin in 1905, which suggests that the Schauman connection may well be right; it also seems to belie the idea that it had some relevance to Sibelius's concern about his health, which was not pinpointed until 1908.

3 : The Later Symphonies
and Symphonic Poems

After the austere and profound searchings to the roots of experience in the Fourth Symphony, Sibelius appeared to turn outwards again in the extrovert Fifth. In this finely energetic composition Sibelius combines the exultant animism of the Second Symphony with the emergence of tragic implications of the Fourth, plus a continuation of the formal dovetailing and synthesizing of the Third. The Fifth is cast in the heroic mould; but its overt heroic quality is tempered, and its musical structure informed by the experience of the stoical Fourth. It is in no way an emotional regression to the Second any more than it is a technical regression to the Third, and to see it as a backward step is as erroneous as to judge the Fourth Symphony of Beethoven a retrogression to the style of the Second.

It was necessary for Sibelius to go through the shadow of the valley of the Fourth before he could re-expand into the Fifth. An immediate starting point might be to see in the Fifth Symphony an upsurge of optimism after the profound pessimism of the Fourth; as, that is, a further extension of the principle of "the conquest of pessimism through art." But such an idea is only tenable within the context of an understanding of the true metaphysical meaning of *optimism* and *pessimism.* The terms do not express the simplistic concept of merely taking a cheerful or despondent view of what life has to offer; instead they represent twin poles of an innermost active principle. It is all too easy to set a kind of negative pessimism against a kind of facile optimism and then to assume that they can be made to cancel each other out: that in the end is meaningless, a hollow evasion. Albert Schweitzer wrote of optimism that it "consists in contemplating and willing the ideal in the light of a deep and self-consistent affirmation of life and the world."* And this again leads on to Nietzsche's concept of "tragic optimism." It is only in this light that the term *optimism* can legitimately be applied to any true work of art. It is certainly the only sense in which it can be applied to the Fifth Symphony of Sibelius, as in a different evolutionary context it can be applied to Beethoven.

Unlike the preceding Fourth Symphony and the succeeding Sixth and Seventh, the Fifth Symphony had to pass through a number of revisions over several years before it found its definitive version. It came out first in 1915, on the occasion of Sibelius's fiftieth birthday, Kajanus conducting. It was, predictably, well received; but it may have been hurried through to meet the date. Whatever the reason it was immediately withdrawn for revision, and reappeared the following year. But still Sibelius was not satisfied and it was again withdrawn. It was then laid aside for three years, and did not again see light of day until Sibelius himself conducted the final edition in November 1919. But by then it had undergone almost complete transformation: the new version was hardly a "revision" at all, but virtually a complete recomposition using the same basic materials.

How far external pressures bear upon the nature and character of works of art is always a difficult, and dangerous conjecture. As well as the fiftieth birthday celebrations, in which it played a central part, the first version of the Fifth Symphony appeared in the year when the darkest implications of the First World War had become evident. At the same time, Sibelius was suffering further deep worry over his health. Given this background, the mood of the symphony can be seen with some justification, as an upsurging optimism in the truest sense, a tragic optimism, a gesture on behalf of life and hope in a time of threatening death and ultimate desolation.

But the Fifth Symphony was not born merely as a heroic riposte—the creative riddle is at once more obstinate and more significant.

In a letter written in 1918 Sibelius spoke of three consecutive symphonies as conceived in a single creative sequence: the recomposed fifth; the sixth, "wild and impassioned"; the seventh, "joy of life and vitality." But it did not work out like that.† If at that time he foresaw

---

*Albert Schweitzer, *Civilization and Ethics* (London: A & C Black, 1946), p. 16.
†It seldom does. At the end of his life Beethoven had plans for at least one new symphony and further Masses, with outlines and sketches. But there is no reason to suppose that had he lived any of them would have come out as projected.

three evolving symphonies that would encompass the totality of his creative force, he added the cautionary note, "All this with due reservation." It was the reservation rather than the outline that in the end prevailed: the grouping was not precisely as he envisaged. The date of the letter is revealing, not because the Great War was nearing its end, but because Sibelius, at this stage was immersed in the recomposition of the Fifth Symphony and in the preliminary sketches for the Sixth, with some anticipations of the Seventh already formulating in his mind. And it is the work of the reconstituted Fifth which gives the key.

If Sibelius in 1918 envisaged three symphonies ahead from the remade Fifth, hindsight suggests that the real significance lies in three back from that central composition. It is probable that that is why the Fifth was obliged to go through such arduous labour pains, pass through its several versions before its proper form and nature could emerge. If that is in fact the case, then the correct grouping of Sibelius's symphonies is: the First and Second standing independently; the Third, Fourth, and Fifth forming a central trilogy; then the Sixth and Seventh again standing independently. This does not of course imply that there is no stylistic or even thematic relationship between the independent works. The creative faculty does not work in isolation, either from aspects of itself or from the rest of the contemporary world. Nor does it mean that the central three are interrelated necessarily in any close or intentional sense; are through-composed, as Beethoven's three *Rasoumovsky* quartets are through-composed in one sense, or his A minor, B flat and C sharp minor late quartets are thematically interconnected via the motif which opens the A minor. All the same, the central three Sibelius symphonies as they stand form a group in stylistic progression and comprehensiveness of content.

The Fourth Symphony remains the pivot work: the Third leads up to it; the Fifth emerges from it. Stylistically, the Third throws a bridge across to the Fifth; the Fourth distills the central essence of both. In both the Third and Fifth, two movements are shunted into one (the last section of the Third, the first of the Fifth); the ultimate in motivic unity and interconnection of cells is represented by the Fourth. The key sequence is also revealing: C major—A minor—E flat. And in both the Third and the Fifth, the middle movement is a kind of intermezzo, a point of thematic and emotional ambivalence.

On its first and second appearances the Fifth Symphony was in four distinct movements.* At this time in point of form and structure, of internal organization that is, it resembled the Fourth rather than the Third. But its essential nature was always nearer to the Third (and back via the Third to the Second in outward appearances†) than to the Fourth. But

---

*The orchestral parts of the first version were discovered after Sibelius's death, and put into a performing edition. Only a few bass parts of the second version survive.

†Performances of the Fifth symphony often refer too directly back to the Second. Koussevitsky's

the musical and aesthetic premises of the Fourth, once worked through, could not be ignored. So, if the Fifth Symphony was to take its place as an emanation of the Fourth, from whatever points of view, it was necessary for it to undergo the kind of clinching process that had wrung the Fourth from the depths of the composer's musical and spiritual being. It did not originally achieve that.

Structurally, the definitive version of the Fifth Symphony carries a stage further the integration of movements of the Third. Again, the most significant movement is bifunctional. In the case of the Third it was the last, which combined the functions of scherzo and finale; in the Fifth it is the first, which combines, in reverse order, those of first movement and scherzo. This leads to some interesting speculations. The Third Symphony begins with a broadly energetic, comparatively straightforward (though subtly organized) movement; passes through an intermediate movement with the character of an intermezzo; then evolves into a large, complex bifunctional (scherzo-cum-finale) conclusion. The Fifth opens with a large, complex bifunctional (first movement-cum-scherzo) design; passes through an intermediate movement with the character of an intermezzo*; then opens out into a broadly conceived, comparatively extrovert finale. Thus the Fourth Symphony, in the overall context, can be seen as "sandwiched" between the two big bifunctional movements of the conclusion of the Third and the opening of the Fifth; becomes in effect the meat in the sandwich of the three-symphony sequence. Or to put it another way, the curve of the graph from the beginning of the Third symphony to the end of the Fifth is thus in the nature of a parabola with the Fourth symphony at the apex.

There is of course no direct warrant for arguing that this design was in the forefront of Sibelius's mind as he composed the three symphonies. It is possible that the difficulties he experienced in finding the right form for the Fifth symphony may have been caused by some intuition that what he first wrote did not accord to the full with the continuity of his symphonic evolution at that particular time. But that still does not mean that he saw the continous process as embracing those three symphonies. Indeed, his letter of 1918 indicates that he saw the recomposed Fifth as the beginning of a cycle, or trilogy, rather than the end of one. Yet hindsight still suggests some validity in seeing the three middle Sibelius symphonies as a group emanating from a complex creative process covering roughly a decade. Whether it was in any sense deliberate or pure coincidence, conscious or unconscious, is neither assessable nor relevant. It simply postulates another way of looking at this period of Sibelius's symphonic

---

classic recording is a case: it has tremendous external vigour and a heroic ring; but it still misses the true essence, the epic quality with all its variety and scope. Unlike the same conductor's unsurpassed Seventh, it takes a too unyielding view.

*That this movement too has a dual aspect—slow movement-scherzando—does not invalidate the central argument: it simply issues a further warning against taking any Sibelius movement at its face value.

work and of throwing light from a different angle onto it. All the same, the more one considers it, the more illuminating does it appear, even if, as Sibelius himself put it when starting the other hare, "All this with due reservation."

Even by Sibelius's own standards the opening movement of the Fifth Symphony is remarkable for its structural integration and unity in diversity. Again, it is built upon the principles of true organic growth which do not so much defy conventional analysis as make it redundant. There is talk about the "double exposition," the "telescoping" of first movement and scherzo, the common derivation of motifs; but it is all largely irrelevant: wherever the blade is slipped in the tissue bleeds because it is organic in the deepest sense and no part can be artificially separated from another without the wound showing. This is not to say that the movement is formless; on the contrary Sibelius, like Beethoven before him was a vindicator of form in music; like Bartók among his contemporaries* and like Wagner in music drama. Viewed in context, it was but an inevitable step forward in symphonic evolution which culminated, as it had to culminate, in the total fusions of the Seventh.

The opening of the Fifth is, as in the Second Symphony, distantly Brahmsian; but now even more than before Brahms transmogrified. The first page is worth quoting in full, for it establishes not only the tone but the genesis of what is to follow,

(See over)

where an embryo theme on horn echoed by bassoons throws off a kind of splinter into the upper woodwind. The latter soon launch themselves onto typically Sibelius semiquaver figurations in thirds which at four after D join with violins in a change of meter and pulse to form a mildly nautical-sounding theme (in G) with a strongly accentuated dotted rhythm:

---

*See "Conclusions."

Within a few more bars a solo trumpet interjects an octave motif, answered by the flute:

Already we have a clutch of motivic cells (there are more too) each one eager to breed or mutate. There is an unmistakable sense of proliferation of life, of nuclei of energy combining and evolving towards some as yet unforeseen end. The so-called repeat of the exposition in no way resembles the eighteenth-century sonata form repeat of sections or periods between double bars; it is more like the multiple growth in plant life where patterns are reproduced as subtle variants of the same inner process of development. On the surface it may sound more or less like the former; internally it is infinitely more subtle and essentially generative.

What is conventionally referred to as the development begins with horns leading to the mournful chanting of a solo bassoon, *lugubre,* which recalls the bleakness and loneliness of the end of the Fourth Symphony. The bassoon's sad song over a rustle of strings broadens into *largamente* and a key change to B major as the initial material briefly reappears.

A glance at the score shows the scherzo section inaugurated by a change of time from 12/8 to 3/4 and a shift to Allegro moderato (*ma poco a poco stretto*). It looks like a clearcut division, a more or less abrupt transition. In fact it has a totally different feel in performance. The running of first movement into scherzo is not achieved by the naïve expedient of simply omitting bars and bar lines; it is brought about through the most complex and subtle fusions and interfertilizations so that in retrospect each part takes into itself basic elements of the other and both emerge as constituent parts of a single unified whole. On paper the end of one section and the beginning of the next is clearly marked; but in fact the whole process is a masterful example of the true art of transition.* The new material that darts out of the time and tempo change is soon revealed as further emanation from what has preceeded it. Yet again, the sense of organic growth, or continuous evolution, through both cellular extension or mutation, is unmistakable. Virtually every thematic motif is a variant of an earlier one. Even the time is interlocked: 3/4 is revealed as a subdivision of 12/8 so that although the pulse alters, the inner mobility does not, since the relationship of bars between sections is simply four to one. Woodwind set off over tremolando strings until again a trumpet chips in with a jaunty

---

*This is the great virtue of Kajanus's recording. With subtle and sensitive use of both tempo and what may be called structural rubato, Kajanus welds the whole together without false emphasis or short breathed conjunctions. Later conductors like Leonard Bernstein and Karajan have achieved similar results by slightly modified means.

theme that suggests it remembered its earlier interjection but was not entirely happy about it. Only when seen as a single evolutionary whole building to the final clinch on E flat in the *presto—più presto* coda, does it make the only kind of sense that justified it, both in itself and in its context, as an integral part of an evolving creative process.

The middle movement has the appearance of an intermezzo, as in the Third Symphony and the Beethoven Fifth, though its musical derivation is more from Beethoven's Seventh via Mendelssohn's *Italian* and in unpremedicated anticipation of Shostakovich's *Leningrad*. After the highly organised and complex dual movement which is the symphony's principal distinction, this unassuming Andante mosso, quasi allegretto may appear almost too inconsequential, as a straightforward set of variations on a theme of impeccable simplicity.

But it is not quite as innocent as it looks. Like the Beethoven Seventh and the *Leningrad*,* it is less variations on a theme than accumulations over a rhythm; and the elements of that rhythm constitute an extended ostinato. The movement is in G major, which links it back to the earlier sections, and in at least two places it shoots tendrils out towards the finale. In character it is not unlike a seemingly bland if civilized conversation which contains behind its undemonstrative surface some sharp reminders and concealed cautions.

It begins with the thematic rhythm in pizzicato strings against sustained octave chords on horns, bassoons and clarinets. This is alternated with characteristic Sibelian thirds and sixths from the flutes. When the strings go over to *arco* it is with a form of divisions, again combined with sustained wind chords. Immediately after C a variant of theme appears on divided violins *poco tranquillo*: it does not stay long, but it too signifies, recurrs, and becomes another informing principle. Thus the primary elements are (a) a thematic rhythm; (b) a woodwind commentary; (c) a modification containing facets of both:

(a)

───────────

*The similarity with the opening of Arnold Bax's Fifth Symphony, dedicated to Sibelius, has been noted. But the tone of the Bax is nothing like Sibelius: it looks forward to Shostakovich and the *Leningrad*, now known to have been conceived in 1938 and later adapted to the siege of Leningrad in 1941. Bax anticipates Shostakovich rather than refering back to Sibelius. The Sibelius connection has been overdone in the case of Bax (and not only Bax among English composers). Bax's symphonic style is far nearer to that of Shostakovich; hardly surprising in view of Bax's strong Russian affiliations.

(b)

(c)

Out of these basic elements a musical structure grows and proliferates. If it may seem upon initial acquaintance to represent Sibelius in a relaxed and even sportive mood, the mistake should not be made of forgetting that it is an integral part of a symphony and assuming that because it is superficially undemanding it actually implies a species of reneging on that intellectual severity and psychological as well as mental concentration, which is the hallmark of his symphonic thinking.

But more than that, at five after F the basses outline the "Thor's hammer" theme of the finale, as well as slightly earlier determining the rhythm confirmed by the timpani behind the tremolando strings at the finale's early pages. This might seem a fairly simplistic unifying device if it began and ended there. But it does not, all through there is internal evidence of that motivic unity and interlocking of ideas which mark the symphonies of Sibelius off from those that rely upon the external linkages familiar in so-called symphonic works superficially held together by crude devices of the *idée fixe* or cyclic interconnection.

Just as the Third Symphony opens with a movement of comparatively forthright physical energy, though highly organized and integrated, so the finale of the Fifth invokes a similar mood to complete the cycle. But because a decade of creative evolution had supervened, with the entire Fourth Symphony as the kernel and central musical and spiritual experience, the focus was sharpened, the perspectives altered. Although again the structure of the finale appears comparatively simple and straightforward, much of the effect derives from the unusual key sequences, which has nothing whatever to do with classical sonata style but is self-generated by the nature of the material and its natural organic evolution—E flat biased towards A, through C major/minor into G flat and back to E flat via the tonic minor. It begins with a kind of *moto perpetuo* of strings *divisi,* picking up woodwind fragments and conjunctions on the way until at D the horns begin the famous hammer theme, minims in thirds:

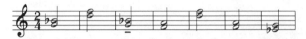

After twenty-five bars this is joined by a longer breathed theme, wood-wind in octaves and cellos in the upper register, at twelve before E:

This moves into C major before a return to E flat brings a modified treatment of the *moto perpetuo* motif. A touch of F major leads to G flat; the above example slips sideways into E flat major before burgeoning forth into a triumphant E flat where it had originally gone into C, and from then onwards opens out into a huge conclusion with great spaced chords reverberating through the orchestra as the argument, the symphony, and the cycle rise to a sonorous ending.

In the Fifth Symphony Sibelius appears to have returned to the unregenerate forces of animate nature. But the naturalism is now much less freely indulged than in the animalistic expansiveness of the Second. The romantic excesses are curbed, if not wholly tamed. Old heroic legends are invoked as answer to the brute passions and violent upsurgings that strode unchallenged through the first two symphonies. The "hero" of the Fifth might even be seen as a latter-day Siegfried who knows nature better than ever the romantic Wagnerian Siegfried knew it: he has lost his illusions, is no longer taken in by notions of a pristine and unsullied nature as the key to all knowledge and wisdom, the panacea for all human woes. Here nature contains dark satanic forces, is the lurking menace and powerful antagonist of the human mind and spirit, destroyer and annihilator if allowed so to be. Yet since man himself is of nature, if also apart from it, he contains within himself the seeds of the conflict, leading potentially to his own destruc-tion. From one point of view this may seem nothing but a variant of the essentially romantic attitude; and so in a sense it is. But it also refers back to primitive man's fears and superstition in the face of natural forces, and his consequent attempts to neutralize it by means of the personalization of gods and animals. And this again is related to the basis of ancient myth and saga to which Sibelius himself was greatly addicted. It was only pinpointed in another form by the romantic movement: it was not invented by romanticism. On the reverse side it gives additional point to Sibelius's proclaimed belief in civilization. His much vaunted affinity with nature, his "nature mystique," was in fact not an identification, as with the romantics, but a confrontation.

To Raymond Bantock,

Jean Sibelius

1907

(Courtesy Music Information Centre, Helsinki)

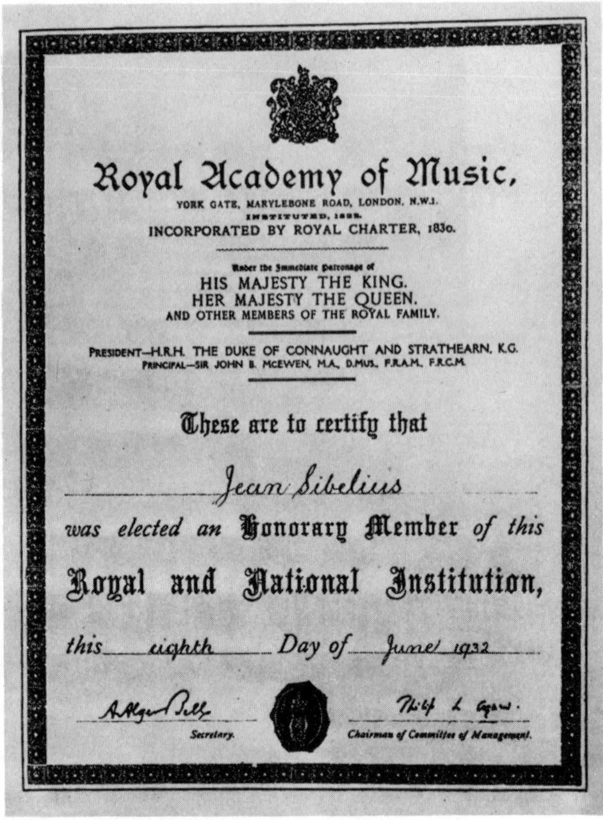

Royal Academy of Music,

YORK GATE, MARYLEBONE ROAD, LONDON, N.W.1.

INSTITUTED, 1822.

INCORPORATED BY ROYAL CHARTER, 1830.

Under the Immediate Patronage of

HIS MAJESTY THE KING.

HER MAJESTY THE QUEEN.

AND OTHER MEMBERS OF THE ROYAL FAMILY.

PRESIDENT—H.R.H. THE DUKE OF CONNAUGHT AND STRATHEARN, K.G.

PRINCIPAL—SIR JOHN B. McEWEN, M.A., D.MUS., F.R.A.M., F.R.C.M.

These are to certify that

Jean Sibelius

was elected an Honorary Member of this

Royal and National Institution,

this eighth Day of June 1932

Secretary.

Chairman of Committee of Management.

Overleaf: Photograph of Sibelius signed by the composer (Courtesy: Raymond Bantock)

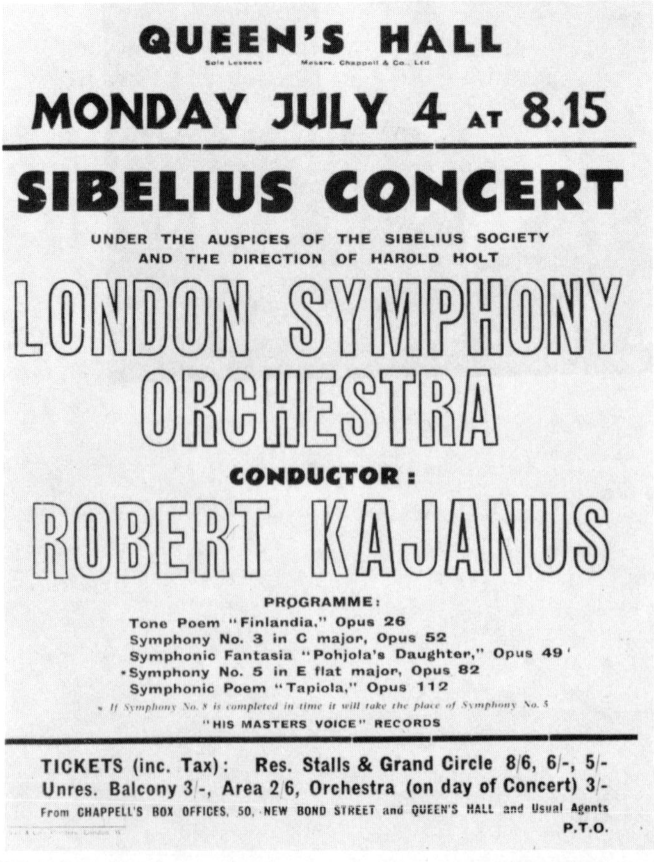

QUEEN'S HALL

Sole Lessees Messrs. Chappell & Co., Ltd.

MONDAY JULY 4 AT 8.15

SIBELIUS CONCERT

UNDER THE AUSPICES OF THE SIBELIUS SOCIETY
AND THE DIRECTION OF HAROLD HOLT

LONDON SYMPHONY ORCHESTRA

CONDUCTOR:

ROBERT KAJANUS

PROGRAMME:

Tone Poem "Finlandia," Opus 26
Symphony No. 3 in C major, Opus 52
Symphonic Fantasia "Pohjola's Daughter," Opus 49
*Symphony No. 5 in E flat major, Opus 82
Symphonic Poem "Tapiola," Opus 112

* *If Symphony No. 8 is completed in time it will take the place of Symphony No. 5*

"HIS MASTERS VOICE" RECORDS

TICKETS (inc. Tax): Res. Stalls & Grand Circle 8/6, 6/-, 5/-
Unres. Balcony 3/-, Area 2/6, Orchestra (on day of Concert) 3/-
From CHAPPELL'S BOX OFFICES, 50, NEW BOND STREET and QUEEN'S HALL and Usual Agents

P.T.O.

Concert programme of 1932 with a reference to the Eighth Symphony (Courtesy Music Information Centre, Helsinki)

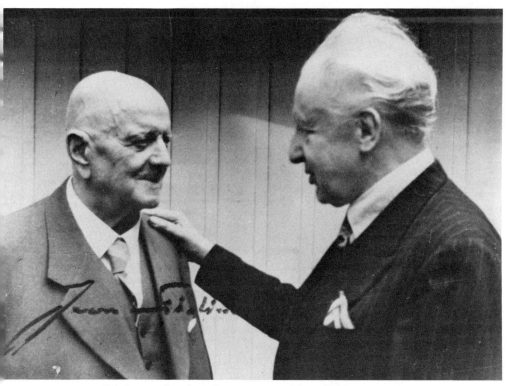

Sibelius and Stokowski (Courtesy: Edward Johnson and the Stokowski estate)

Sibelius and Sir Thomas Beecham (Courtesy: Music Information Centre, Helsinki)

After the stoical glimpse into the abyss of the Fourth Symphony, the Fifth returns its heroic challenge. But it is the hostility of natural forces that lies behind both. Such, in a nutshell, is the fundamental difference between a nineteenth-century and a twentieth-century consciousness, between, that is, a romantic and a scientific life- and world-view. It is also one reason why the first two symphonies and some other works are seen as old fashioned, romantically indulgent, while the later ones are admissable into the contemporary ethic and aesthetic. It is a superficial view, as I have shown; but it is understandable from a certain point of view. Sibelius came out of the late nineteenth century into the twentieth, emerging as did the historical process itself, from one age into another, harder and more uncompromising. The cycle of the three central symphonies is in many respects the record of that emergence.

With that aesthetic and existential experience behind him, Sibelius did not so much change direction as alter the bias of his responses. Externally, the Sixth Symphony, being cast in four separate movements with close motivic interlocking, appears to return to the formal principles of the Fourth, while its undemonstrative, often ambiguous tone seems to return to the Third. In fact it is not in any meaningful sense, a return to either. After the complex of experiences worked through in the Third, Fourth, and Fifth symphonies, Sibelius's evolving creative faculty could go in several different directions. Its particular constitution led it in that of the Sixth Symphony. That it was not preordained is shown by the marked difference between it as it actually emerged and the tentative preliminary description of it in the letter of 1918. "Wild and impassioned. Sombre with pastoral contrasts. Probably in four movements with the end rising to a sombre roaring in the orchestra, in which the main theme is drowned." As it turned out, little remained but the "four movements"; everything else in the initial prospectus, so to say, was utterly transformed, suffered strange, and only in part foreseeable, changes.

Alban Berg spoke of the Sixth Symphony of Gustav Mahler, which appeared in 1905, as "the only Sixth, the *Pastoral* notwithstanding." Berg either overlooked or was not acquainted with the Sixth Symphony of Sibelius, a no less remarkable and original composition from, as usual, the opposite standpoint. In certain respects the Sixth symphonies of Sibelius and Mahler pinpoint the essential opposition between their respective views of the symphony, for the introduction of voices into several of Mahler's symphonies serves only to diffuse rather than clarify the central argument. In the Sixth Symphony, which appeared in 1923, Sibelius carried his own symphonic evolution as well as that of the symphony in the twentieth century yet one stage further in thematic interlocking and motivic unity, in contradistinction to Mahler, who, in his Sixth, expanded and confirmed his own principles of inclusiveness and the all-embracing, filling it with autobiographical content, the picturesque (cow-bells), the symbolic (hammer blows), the elaborate and existentially soul-searching, especially in the problematic and complex finale.*

Outwardly, the Sixth Symphony of Sibelius appears to refer back to the Fourth, with its four separate but thematically, or motivically, interrelated movements. And this is true enough, so long as one recognizes that the fusion of two or more movements into one and the inter-connection of otherwise independent movements through common motifs and thematic modules is all part of the same creative process.

The Sixth Symphony immediately establishes two principles: its undemonstrative tone and the prominence of modality. In fact neither of these are in any way exceptional, even unusual, in Sibelius. It used to be held† that the modal inflexions were somthing new and unexpected, a legacy of a late-life study, as with Beethoven, of the sixteenth-century polyphonists. In fact, the tendency to modal melody and harmony had been a feature of Sibelius's music from the beginning. It is hinted at in *Kullervo,* has clear implications in *The Swan of Tuonela* and the First Symphony, and crops up, either explicitly or by implication all through his career. In the Sixth Symphony it is simply brought to the fore, emphasized, in a sense spotlighted, just as in *The Oceanides* Sibelius exploits certain aspects of his orchestration that were always present but had not previously been erected into a primary element. But the fundamental idiom of the Sixth remains indelibly Sibelian. The scoring has two significant points: firstly, like Mahler (and it is about the only point where Mahler and Sibelius meet on any ground) though the instrumental forces are comprehensive, requiring here double woodwind, additional trumpet, bass clarinet and harp, the use made of them is restrained, often reduced to virtual chamber proportions. Secondly, the extensive exploitation of strings recalls *Rakastava,* and the inclusion of the harp picks up where *The Bard* took initial shape. Since technically both *The Bard* and *Rakastava* relate to the Fourth Symphony, here is a further linkage between that masterpiece and this later one.

The Sixth Symphony is sometimes stated as being in D Minor, although the score does not specify any key signature. The Dorian mode is established at the outset, in the polyphonic opening for strings. More than with the Fifth Symphony the opening pages of the Sixth require quoting in score.

At an immediate glance this might suggest part of the A minor String Quartet of Beethoven, the "Heilige Dankgesang" in particular. A

---

*Mahler's deletion of the dreaded third hammer blow in the finale would never have occurred to Sibelius, the least superstitious of men and musicians, however he may have invoked ancient gods and legends. This marks another major distinction between the two and may constitute another reason why Mahler, though liking the man Sibelius detested his music.

†By Cecil Gray in particular.

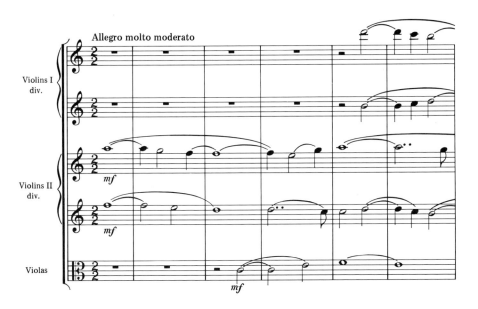

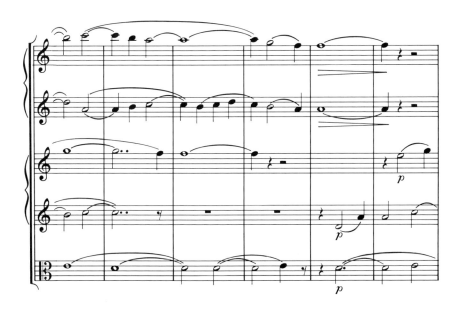

second cursory look might intimate something out of Bruckner. Both are significant. The influence of Beethoven on Sibelius, whatever it precisely was, need hardly be insisted upon; but that of Bruckner raises, and perhaps abides, another question.

While he was in Vienna as a young man, Sibelius heard and was much impressed by the symphonies of Bruckner. Subsequently his treatment of the sections of the orchestra owed something to Bruckner's practice in inverse relation to what it did not owe to Mahler's. And in 1911 Sibelius wrote in a letter that he had recently heard a performance of Bruckner's Fifth Symphony that has "moved me to tears." A "strangely profound spirit," Sibelius saw in Bruckner, "formed by a religious sense," which he then felt to be "no longer in harmony with our time." It would not be possible to equate the Sixth Symphony of Sibelius with any music by Anton Bruckner: for one thing, and apart from the religious instigation, the Brucknerian time-scale was as far apart from the Sibelian as the Sibelian was apart from the Mahlerian inclusiveness/exclusiveness or selectivity. Nor was motivic unity a marked feature of Bruckner's symphonic processes. On the surface therefore nothing would seem to be farther apart than a symphony by Sibelius and one by Bruckner. Yet it is possible to see an internal, if obverse relationship. If the symphonies of Bruckner represent a profound, unquestioning affirmation of faith, those of Sibelius, and especially the Fourth are the outcome of a no less profound, essentially questioning sense of lost or broken faith. But the recognition of lost or broken faith at least postulates the former existence of faith, whereas a total rejection or nihilistic negation cannot admit its former existence or must assert that it was nothing but illusion, blind superstition, and did not therefore constitute a point of genuine reaction. In a sense too, this determines the physical attributes of the respective symphonies: an affirmation of faith implies expansion, a sense of loss or breaking of it equally tends towards contraction.

The quietism of the Sixth Symphony is first of all the consequence of its musical material; but that material itself is a reflection of Sibelius's state of mind and spirit at the time of its composition, four years that is (in its final form) after the completion of the definitive version of the Fifth Symphony, and thus the conclusion of the central symphonic cycle. Its quietism is not that of, say, the Vaughan Williams *Pastoral* any more than it is that of Beethoven's. It has been called Sibelius's "Pastoral"; but in fact its nature affinity is no more than that of the other symphonies, and its pastorality less than that of parts of the Second. Its premises are more spiritual than natural, its quality both human and legendary, as musically established by its relationship to *Rakastava* and *The Bard*. These particular qualities are further emphasized by the relative tempi of the four movements, each specifically qualified: Allegro molto moderato—Allegretto moderato—Poco vivace—Allegro molto. Even the final movement—hardly a finale in the powerfully clinching sense, whether fast or slow—is restrained, its pace less lithe and quick-footed than the marking might infer. Also remarkable are the continual rhythmic complexities (again as unostentatious as unmistakable) that underpin the melodic polyphony. Throughout, everthing is subtle, slanted, rich in concentrated thought, reticent in tone of voice or exertion of muscle.

Such is the character of the Sixth Symphony. In point of musical construction and organization it is often so subtle, so elusive,* that formal analysis is defeated by lack of any familiar signposts or clear thematic evolution. This of course is nothing new in Sibelius; but here it is carried to farther extremes in extreme directions. (This does not in any sense imply that the music is formless; simply that, as before, it obeys laws of its own constitution, the form generated by the material, but since the material is elusive and the constitution, though internally robust, the opposite of squarecut and straightforward, the form cannot be separated from either.)

If the overall argument were not so cogent, the interrelationship between sections so close throughout, it might be said that the weight was thrown onto the outer movements; that the musical density, or specific gravity, of the Sibelius Sixth resembled the $1 + 1(2) + 1 = 3$ of the Beethoven Eighth. And to some extent it would be justified. The first movement and finale certainly appear to form a frame for the two middle ones; and first movement and finale have the closest thematic interlocking. Also, both middle movements have a somewhat ambivalent character, neither definitely one thing nor another: certainly the second is no more a slow movement than the corresponding movement of the Beethoven Eighth; and the third, usually referred to as "Scherzo," is again ambiguous with its half suppressed muscularity and hints of extrovert power that never fully materialize, even when the brass are momentarily given their head. In all four movements the familiar (too familiar) Sibelian rhetoric is missing. This has led some to infer that the Sixth Symphony is pale, even a devitalized reflection of the big-boned "masculine" Sibelius; but this is an insensitive, "one eyed" view.

It was the Sixth Symphony that prompted Sibelius's other famous riposte to the goings on in the musical world of the time. As the Fourth Symphony was issued as a "protest against contemporary compositions" with "nothing of the circus about it," so he said of the Sixth that while other composers provided highly spiced cocktails, he offered "pure spring water." Although it would be an exaggeration to see the Sixth Symphony as a cold douche and generally sobering libation in an otherwise heady and overheated musical world, much the same arguments apply as with the Fourth and its "protest."

---

*It is so elusive that very few conductors have come anywhere near penetrating its essence. Kajanus did not record it; Schneevoigt did, but unlike his fascinating and highly individual Fourth, which Sibelius did not like but which reveals many unusual facets of that great work, the Sixth is rushed and insensitive. Beecham's recording, preferred by Sibelius himself, although issued on HMV 78s in 1948, originated with RCA and so cannot be included in the invaluable historical series from World Records, an EMI subsidiary. Of the later conductors, Karajan comes nearest in both his recordings—on mono Columbia with the Philharmonia, and on stereo DGG with the Berlin Philharmonic—or Colin Davis on Philips.

After the polyphonic, nonthematic opening of the first movement, for divided strings joined after twenty seven bars by woodwind and later by sustained brass chords, an embryonic theme appears on flutes in thirds repeated by oboes ditto, at B:

This has been designated "first subject"; and so it might be if such nomenclature had any real meaning in the context. The movement thereafter evolves according to its own laws of development, and they are the laws which Sibelius had established in outline, though not in detail, in previous symphonies. The decisive factor is the continual bias towards the Dorian mode. The material progresses by a form of thematic mutation by which the nuclei are transformed by internal organic evolution so that each successive aspect of the material appears as an internal organic emanation of what has gone before, and what is to come. This is the process by which the entire symphony grows and evolves, the finale clinching the hypotheses of the first movement by interior reference.

The second movement, like that of the Fifth Symphony, is deceptive in its apparent simplicity; but unlike that movement it rises to no climax but proceeds in a kind of persistent understatement. It begins with soft syncopated wind chords out of which the strings inaugurate the search for a theme, starting:

The working out can hardly be described as variations; but as in the corresponding movement of the Fifth it tends to proceed by a form of divisions, the process consolidated at G by a quickening of the pulse and an intricate passage for strings in semiquavers which carries along with it a wind motif already introduced and again thematically generating. The movement ends, on a Dorian plagal cadence, like the Fourth Symphony's scherzo, peremptorily, with a sudden snapping off at a point where the ear anticipates some further elucidation of the matter in hand.*

---

*To return to a former analogy, Hemingway too would often end a story, even a novel, with a sudden sharp cryptic phrase or sentence.

The third movement, called "Scherzo" though not on the score, is the most reminiscent of the four. It sets off with a galloping motif in dotted rhythm which appears to derive directly from *Lemminkäinen's Return* and the ride section of *Nightride and Sunrise* with an associated wind figure; and rushing string passages plus a chorale-like theme on the woodwind (at C), both of which recall the finale of the Fourth Symphony. The galloping motif (a) dominates; the chorale (b) both alternates and contrasts with it:

(a)

(b)

The structure is typical of Sibelius's way of "shunting" symphonic form; everything is foreshortened, cryptic almost. Big brass chords sound, the only place in the whole symphony where the voice is raised. But nothing comes of it. The Sixth Symphony, like the Fourth, particularly in the scherzo and finale, leaves the listener wondering all the time what has been left out, but certain that Sibelius knew precisely what.

The finale is full of hints and suggestions rather than plain statements. It begins with a fresh form of the first bars of the first movement, which are now revealed as containing what has been called the *Kärnmotiv* or germ cell of the entire symphony, the primary unit out of which all four movements directly or indirectly grow and from which the all-pervading descending sequences derive. The opening of the finale exposes this motif via chorale-like antiphonies between wind and *divisi* violins in alternation with lower strings. In these opening bars is the thematic germination of the whole movement and the linking back through cross reference to the first movement, then back again via the middle two. Not even in the Fourth Symphony was thematic integration and motivic unity within and across four apparently distinct movements so close-knit or so subtly organized. Even motifs which seem unrelated on their first appearance turn out to be offshoots, mutations, mirror inversions or by-products of something else. The recurrent rhythmic figure in the main body of the finale, rounded off on successive appearance by the timpani, at first produces one of Sibelius's by now familiar enigmatic effects—until one realizes that behind the drum taps is an entirely different area of the argument which has been deliberately left out.

Certain commentators, influenced no doubt by the subdued tone and colours, and perhaps missing the full implications of the omissions, have seen the Sixth Symphony as essentially serene, even placid. And so in a sense it is, relatively speaking. It is not an embattled or proselytizing composition: it appears outwardly to assert no imperatives, argue from no direct hypotheses. It contains, as all symphonic works of consequence must in one form or another, the seeds of conflict, but it does not cultivate them assiduously or propound resonant answers. Yet if peace appears to be won, even "peace with honour," it is more in the nature of an armistice than an ultimate transcendance. If the Fourth Symphony in one of its existential and metaphysical aspects and the necessary musical corollaries, is a symphony of disillusion, the Sixth suggests, not a return to faith, for there was none in the contemporary context to return to—it is nothing like the Bruckner Fifth which had so moved Sibelius in 1911—yet it may still perhaps be seen as a point of relative repose in a hostile world and in the context of Sibelius's own spiritual and artistic evolution. And in the latter context it marks yet one more significant and necessary advance.

Like so many subtle, enigmatic, frequently elusive compositions, especially in the catalogue of one generally known for the large gesture and the powerful, not to say stentorian tone of voice, the Sixth Symphony has always been underrated and usually misunderstood and misconstrued. Not so the Seventh, which has all over been recognized as a remarkable and original work of no mean stature, if not always for impeccable reasons. Even Sibelius himself does not appear to have been quite certain about it at first. The letter of 1918 speaks of "The VII Symphony Joy of life and vitality, with *appassionato* passages. In three movements—the last a Hellenic rondo." But again it did not come out like that. As with the Sixth, in the half dozen years that supervened, considerable changes of direction came about. In the end the Seventh Symphony emerged as a single continuous, totally integrated structure; not just three or four sections rolled up and parcelled into one by devices either strange or ingenious, or both, but a genuinely evolving organism without seams or arbitrary shifts of texture or tissue. It was originally promoted and presented as "Symphonic Fantasia"; only later did Sibelius admit it into the canon of the symphonies proper. It was almost as though, looking at the complete score, he was momentarily nonplussed by what he had done and needed the "moment of truth" of actual performance to convince himself that it really was what he meant, and how he meant it.

Of the original scheme something this time remains; more than with the Sixth, though not in form or structure. Joy of life and vitality; yes, it is there, even if it is never paraded; *appassionato* passages, and yes, again, at times and with the same qualification. But of the three movements originally proposed nothing remains; and the "Hellenic rondo" (whatever that was supposed to have been) has gone the way of all ideas that jump in the artistic mind but then sink back without producing the germinating spark. All the same, it is possible to feel in the Seventh something of that Greek spirit with which Sibelius always felt a close affinity, increasingly as he grew older. Its lofty tone, the vivid energies of the *vivacissimo* and *presto* sections, suggesting perhaps some forms of the Greek games and certainly full of "joy of life and vitality," though that need not necessarily apply to quick sections only. In view of Sibelius's expressed view that he saw "classicism as the way of the future" and his lifelong addiction to Greek culture, it may not be too fanciful to see in the Seventh Symphony his most complete and idealized achievement of the Greek ideal of the conquest of pessimism through art. The catastrophic trombone theme suggests that the conquest in this of its many forms was entirely necessary.

On the plain musical side one of the first things to strike home about the Seventh Symphony, apart of course from its form and structure, is that it justifies Schoenberg's contention that there is still a great deal of good music to be written in C major. At the same time, no one coming to the Seventh Symphony and seeing "in C Major" written on the score will be taken in to supposing that a straightforward piece of clearcut classical, C major tonality is to be expected. Beethoven when he said C major meant precisely that: he may have dallied or strayed along the way; but he set out from C and to that unequivocally is where he returned. But in the post-*Tristan* musical world, and in the Schoenbergian world, nothing could ever again be taken for granted, whether in Debussy, Stravinsky, or even Richard Strauss—and certainly not in Sibelius. Thus the Seventh Symphony, though in C major, is tonal in a twentieth-not an eighteenth-century sense and manner. The rising scale on C which launches the symphony lands on a chord of A flat. Most curious, as Berlioz might have said.

There were a number of attempts during the nineteenth century to achieve a fusion and integration of the separate sonata form movements, from Schubert's *Wanderer Fantasia* through Liszt's B minor sonata down to Schoenberg in the first years of the twentieth. Thus Sibelius's tackling of the problem was hardly unique, and not even spankingly original. But it was unusual in two ways: firstly it was applied to full-scale orchestral symphony with the motivic unity and interlocking that is necessary to true symphonic thinking and which Sibelius himself understood and

honoured. Secondly, the manner of that fusion and integration was far
more subtle and went much farther than anything so far attempted on a
large scale. It was total fusion rather than the simple expedient used
previously by other composers of introducing common themes or motifs
into different movements, of juggling with bridge passages, or running
together things that are quite obviously separate, to create an impression of
continuity. Sibelius himself had even done this in the Second Symphony;
but all he did there was to run the end of the scherzo into the beginning of
the finale by a simple process of "opening out"—a change of internal
movement but no organic process in any meaningful sense. It was hardly
more, in itself, and leaving aside the motivic unity through the whole
symphony, than our old familiar the *attacca subito,* a device not unknown to
composers for at least two hundred years previously.

The organic fusion and continuity of the Seventh Symphony renders
formal analysis particularly difficult. Whereas with the Third through the
Sixth the insertion of the scalpel of analysis of themes, counterthemes,
generic motifs, and structural procedures, causes the texture and tissue to
bleed, in the case of the Seventh it simply snaps the blade off. Much of the
writing is polyphonic with modal inflexions, though it is possible to argue
in a more general sense that Sibelius was not a natural polyphonic
composer but one who used polyphony for specific purposes in specific
contexts. And again, the Seventh Symphony is a further extension of
Sibelius's achievement as a vindicator of form, in that here form and
content are completely indivisible, the physical form and structure of
the whole work entirely generated by the material and the underlying
thought-processes not in parts but all through, beginning to end.

Yet this is only the consummation of a process that was always
inherent; a final form of the motivic unity of the four outwardly separate
movements of the Fourth and Sixth symphonies and the fusion of sections
in the Third and Fifth. And it may well be that in the ultimate integration
of the Seventh Symphony, Sibelius to a certain extent spiked his own guns.
Having once achieved, initially so it appears to his own momentary
perplexity, if not discomfiture, that consummation, he could not bring
himself, either psychologically or aesthetically, to break it down again into
something like its constituent parts. We do not know what form the
mythical "Eighth" Symphony took, or tried to take; whether it was to have
been in separate movements or a further extension of total integration,
perhaps from a different standpoint, or maybe some admixture of the two
as in the Third and Fifth; but the logical deduction is that, whichever it
was, what he had already done rendered it redundant to his always acute
sense of self-criticism. It is from this point of view perhaps that it may be
said that for Sibelius after the Seventh Symphony symphonic form was a
worked out mine. Lacking a sight of the score of the Eighth Symphony,
such as it may have been it is impossible to reach any more decisive
assessment.

Since conventional analysis of the Seventh Symphony can only have the effect of breaking apart what was intended to remain an indissoluble unity, and quotation of themes inevitably concentrate on the obvious or "juicy" bits,* it is probably best to attempt no more than a broad description of the music's evolutionary progress. Nowhere in Sibelius do scraps of theme and pieces of texture "breed" more prolifically; nowhere are the internal relationships tighter or more subtly organized. Time and again minute thematic or rhythmic fragments subsequently reveal themselves as true motivic nuclei, generic units of energy essential to the long-term cohesion of the structure. Despite the concentration, the variety of movement and rhythmic dexterity, the time-scale is nearer to that of Wagner than Haydn, or even Beethoven. Once again it is what is left out as much as what is put in that gives the music its essential character and its sense of size and scope within a comparatively short physical space. Exclusion rather than inclusion is hardly a Wagnerian precept. But that is not the point: it is the implied not the explicit dimension that matters.

Just as the *leitmotiven* technique of Wagner has been grossly over-played and overestimated, so the habit of winkling out "subjects" has led to distortions of their real function in the later symphonies of Sibelius. In both cases too much attention has been paid to the facts, too little to either their origins or their real consequences. Recurrence of "leading motifs" in Wagner or "themes" in Sibelius do not mean what they meant in classical sonata form, still less what they failed to mean in postclassical music misconceived in classical terms.

From the beginning Sibelius showed himself master of pace and movement in music. His slow music is intrinsically different from his quick music; it is not simply the same music with a different tempo marking. Neither Brahms nor Bruckner fully mastered this difficult art. In the true classical style as consolidated by Mozart and Haydn and extended by Beethoven, this was seldom a problem because the forms themselves tended to determine pace and movement; but it became one when the existential context altered and composers of the romantic movement tried to force new wine into old bottles, frequently referring back to the forms of mid-period Beethoven which Beethoven himself had outgrown. This is one of the major problems of the post-Beethoven symphony, and it is so because in the classical style (and not only in music) form and proportion are uppermost whereas in the romantic aesthetic content is all-important, and left to itself the equation simply

---

*As so often, Donald Tovey put it best, "An adequate analysis of this noble work would be too *subtle to be readable; and the listener would probably find its points more evident in the music than* in any words." *Essays in Musical Analysis* (London: Oxford University Press, 1939) 6:91

will not come out.* Sibelius, with his strongly intellectual bent and his consequent acute sense of form, understood this, recognized the necessity of evolving new forms and structures to encompass the existential pressures of the modern evolutionary consciousness. He was not of course the only one so to do—Schoenberg was also faced with the same kind of problem and was obliged to solve it through a transformation of the basic language of music after realizing that post-Wagnerian chromaticism was as played out as sonata form and like it belonged to another era of creative evolution. Schoenberg solved it one way, Sibelius another, each according to his own temperament and his own creative responses.

All this is pertinent to the Seventh Symphony. It is impossible to achieve genuine organic growth in an extended musical composition without real rather than simulated changes of pace and movement, or without a true sense of internal development; otherwise all that ensues is either an amorphous texture which makes irrelevant gestures or a succession of loosely related sections cleverly or clumsily stitched together. That in neither case is this true of the Sibelius Seventh has long been recognized; the only trouble is that conventional analysis persists in suggesting the opposite effect, inevitably, and so is best avoided.

The symphony emerges from darkness into light via the long rising scale passage beginning on lower strings and ending on A flat. Sibelius shared with Beethoven something which Wagner erected into a leading principle—a way of consciously making the unconscious articulate. The opening pages of the Seventh Symphony seem to emerge out of the unconscious. The scale motif is an important initiation, an integral part of the overall structure. It is immediately followed by a motif for woodwind, again important but most so for the little tag at the end

immediately followed by a descending four-note motif (oboes), both of which turn out to be primary nuclei. There then follows an extended polyphonic passage, modally inflected which partially recalls the Sixth Symphony, until at seven after C the great trombone theme appears, its second half referring to the rising scale of the opening:

(See over)

---

*This does not of course in any way imply that classical music is without deep content or that romantic music is necessarily without meaningful form. Maybe it can be simplified by saying that classical values are primarily social while romantic values are primarily individual. This can lead to rigid formalism on the one hand and blatant egocentricity on the other, but is generally a matter of bias and emphasis rather than dogma.

A conventional analysis can see these first ninety-two bars (to four before F) as an exposition leading into forty-one bars of development. This is all very well; but the so-called exposition is already developmental and what follows is simply an extension of the same basic process. At three after F strings have a clear anticipation of the theme of the *vivacissimo* (at J), often referred to as the first scherzo. This latter moves with exceptional energy and genuine pace, a darting, stabbing motion which ends in running crochets in the strings as the pace slackens to return to *adagio* at L with the first reappearance of the trombone theme, now supported by horns and bassoon over running quavers in the strings taken up by the bassoons at M. A change of key and tempo, to allegro molto moderato, at thirteen after N, introduces what at first appear to be new motifs, but are not: they are further mutations of those from the exposition, including the trombone theme. This evolves after some working up into a second scherzo, moving through *vivace* with much use of a motif derived from the rising scale via the second part of the trombone theme, and ending *presto* in propulsive agitation until the return to *adagio* at four after X brings a final appearance of the trombone theme and then moves to a huge climax, *largamente* with the descending four-note motif from the opening pages prominent and the symphony ends, *affetuoso,* with a consolatary skeleton of the trombone theme on solo flute and solo bassoon over tremolando strings, and then the sonorous closing bars, sustained wind and strings, tempo I *f* to *ff*.

Temptations in the wilderness! Sibelius himself is quoted by Ralph Hill in the Abraham Symposium as saying, "You know how the wing of a butterfly crumbles at a touch? So it is with my compositions; the very mention of them is fatal." Outlining the progress of the Seventh Symphony, is indeed a temptation to be resisted, for there is no way in which one can even mention changes of tempi, cue letters, themes isolated from the total texture, let alone such shifty expedients as exposition, development, recapitulation, without giving a sectional impression of what is essentially continuous, organic, all of a piece.

Concurrently with the Seventh Symphony Sibelius was working on the last and greatest of his symphonic tone poems, *Tapiola*. * This, like *The Oceanides,* was written to a commission from America, from Walter Damorsch who gave it in New York at the very end of 1926. *Tapiola* has sometimes been called a symphony in all but name;† but the whole point about *Tapiola* is that it is not a symphony: placed alongside the Seventh Symphony it finally establishes the difference between the two genres, a difference and distinction which Sibelius maintained all his life and which defined the polarities of his specific contribution to the music of the emergence of the twentieth century out of the remnants of the nineteenth.

Tapiola has been recognized as essentially monothematic and as the ultimate extension of Sibelius's unique treatment of the orchestra. Both assessments are correct; but both are susceptible to misinterpretation. Certainly, however many themes or motifs may be quoted, every one derives from the principal one which appears in the first three bars:

This, it should by now be self-evident, is in accord with Sibelius's standard practice. Although the symphonies usually contain several ger-minative motifs, the basic material is nearly always related to one central thematic nucleus, however distantly at a preliminary hearing, or inspec-tion. *Tapiola,* being a tone poem and not a symphony, reduces the process to a single nucleus; but the subsequent working out by no means relies upon repetition and simple variation. No less than in the symphonies but from its inherently different standpoint, *Tapiola* exposes the central Sibelian principle of achieving the utmost variety within the utmost unity, of that internal interlocking and organic fusion which sets him apart from all the romantic symphonists and most postromantic ones too.

In the Seventh Symphony Sibelius achieved the final synthesis of symphonic thinking; in *Tapiola* he did the same for symphonic poem. And in *Tapiola* too he achieved his most masterful handling of the orchestra, infusing it with devices and effects latent in the symphonies, most notably the Sixth and Seventh, but stemming from the central trilogy, but for which there was little opportunity for total exploration in that essentially nonillustrative context. Technically, as well as spiritually and intellectu-ally the Seventh Symphony and *Tapiola* can only be fully understood

---

*Although the Seventh Symphony appeared in 1924 and *Tapiola* two years later, it is clear that both were in Sibelius's mind at the same time. The internal evidence demonstrates it even more decisively than the external circumstances.

†By Ernest Newman originally. Yet even without the brief programatic quotation, *Tapiola* would still make the same effect, both emotionally and musically—an effect quite different from that produced by a symphony.

through their intimate inter-relationship. If the central three symphonies as a kind of trilogy may be an argument not universally and immediately acceptable, the cross-references between the Seventh Symphony and *Tapiola* can hardly be mistaken or misconstrued even in the farthest reaches of inattention. If the Seventh Symphony pushes symphonic synthesis to its extremes, *Tapiola* pushes orchestral technique and effectiveness in their unique Sibelian terms to the same limits. The use of internal ostinati and sustained organ points deep in the orchestra, the inimitable writing for woodwind and brass, unmistakable from a single bar, the sheer sound of the strings—all these have their precedents in the earlier works; but in *Tapiola* they achieve a magnificent apotheosis.

Ubiquitously quoted though they are, the four lines from the *Kalavela* that preface the score of *Tapiola* remain relevant:

> Wide-spread they stand, the Northland's dusky forests,
> Ancient, mysterious, brooding savage dreams,
> Within them dwells the Forest's mighty God,
> And wood-sprites in the gloom weave magic spells.

The coexistence of the heroic affirmation of the Seventh Symphony in an entirely humanistic, nonreligious contemporary context, and the tone poem in which the ferocity of hostile nature is more uncompromisingly expressed than anywhere else in music, even by Sibelius himself, has its own significance. *Tapiola* is one of the most completely ferocious and deliberately inimical compositions in existence. If we ask what precisely it is, in the mind and consciousness of Sibelius, that man is up against, and over which he has ultimately to establish dominance, both within and outside himself, if he is not only to prevail but even to survive, we need look no farther than *Tapiola.* The "savage dreams" Sigmund Freud uncovered in the unconscious here break out into articulate menace. There are musical compositions which send agreeable shivers down the spine; but as often as not they are of the turnip and candle variety: like the "Witches' Sabbath" in the *Symphonie fantastique* of Berlioz, they make scarifying faces but break no bones. *Tapiola* is another matter—it rocks the foundations of human composure; shatters the last remnants of complacency.

Even more than with the Seventh Symphony, an analytical commentary on *Tapiola* would only demonstrate its own irrelevance. More than any other Sibelius work *Tapiola* is a "one off." Although at a certain level it has its antecedents in earlier compositions, it is a supreme example of one specific mode of expression evolved for one specific purpose, and it could only have come into being as the end product of a long and continuous process of creative evolution in the mind of one man.

The idea that Sibelius's "nature music" (and on this assessment that means most of it) represents a progression towards total submergence into nature of the human personality cannot be maintained. It is in this sense too that the Fourth Symphony has to be seen as the pivot work in Sibelius's career. It was possible for Sibelius before the Fourth Symphony to ride on the back of natural animism, to exult in its elemental energy and vitality while remaining aware of its menace. But the lonely and desolate cry at the end of the Fourth Symphony is a kind of valediction, not only for Sibelius himself but for mankind in the modern scientific world, for Western man anyway; a farewell not only to the dream of the romantics but to all the comforting assumptions on which humankind had built its edifices, however shaky; to the sense of oneness with the natural world which had become the corollary of religious experience when belief in oneness with God had been declined, and is in fact what is frequently taken to be Sibelius's own attitude as a form of "nature mysticism." Sibelius was too honest a man and artist to take refuge in any form of substitute religion, and after the Fourth Symphony for him submergence of the personality in nature was no longer a possibility. Rather it was the exact opposite: a constant reinforcing of the human mind and will, the strengthening of the personality in the face of natural hostility; the profound sense of the human spirit in a hostile environment. Just how hostile is revealed in *Tapiola,* the implication confirmed by the resolution at the end of the tone poem and the heroic affirmation of the Seventh Symphony's closing bars.

For the later Sibelius, whatever may have been the case in the days of his rampageous youth and young manhood, the destiny of man was not to be fulfilled, the wound healed, by immersion in and identification with the world of nature or some vague idea of the cosmos, as the romantics thought. *Tapiola* affirms, as the Fourth Symphony intimated and much that came after it confirmed, not oneness or identification with but contemporary civilized man's alienation from nature.

4 : *Sibelius and the Theatre*

It is generally agreed that Sibelius ended his active career (apart from work on the Eighth Symphony) with the Seventh Symphony and *Tapiola,* and that after those two masterpieces no substantial music emerged. In fact this is only two-thirds true: Sibelius did not end with a pair of late masterpieces, but with three; for besides his most advanced evolution of symphonic form and the greatest of his symphonic poems there was also his finest score for the theatre, the incidental music to the 1926 Copenhagen production of Shakespeare's *The Tempest*.

From the outset Sibelius was strongly drawn to the theatre. Quite early on he declared a belief in almost Wagnerian terms, that music only fully realizes itself in association with words. It was probably sometime after the withdrawal of *Kullervo* that he either changed his mind or decided not to act on that belief. All his life he wrote for the human voice. He was an accomplished composer of solo songs; and the list of his works for mixed voices is formidable, even if it contains few that significantly advance his reputation. Yet he wrote no opera–or none to speak of. His one act *The Maiden in the Tower* was obviously nothing special, and the projected *The Building of the Boat,* apart from the masterly *The Swan of Tuonela* originally planned as its prelude, never went beyond the stage of sketches. Sibelius's contributions to the theatre consist of incidental music to ten plays of varying sorts—an occupation at which he was adept. He clearly had a strong theatrical sense, and in his youth at least was a familiar figure at theatre productions and the opera. Yet the bald fact remains that, after those two early and more or less abortive forays, he never again seriously addressed himself to the operatic form.

Precisely why Sibelius never turned his hand to opera or music drama after the abortive essays from the 1890s, is not entirely clear. With his strong dramatic sense and highly individual way of writing for voices, plus his lifelong addiction to Finnish legend and mythology, classical literature and contemporary drama, it may at first seem peculiar. But perhaps the answer is simpler, and in the end not very mysterious. Most post-Beethoven composers who worked principally in symphony or the larger instrumental forms—Brahms, Bruckner, Mahler, Bax, Elgar—more or less assiduously avoided the opera (as composers, that is; Mahler of course was one of the great opera conductors), while the opera composers—Wagner, Verdi, Puccini, many smaller fry, mostly Italian—did virtually nothing else. It may just be that a creative faculty that moves positively in one direction does not move equally positively in the other. The Russians in some respects constitute a partial exception; but then the Russians tend to be exceptions to everything.* Perhaps Beethoven himself, a natural symphonic thinker in music who struggled long and manfully to fashion an opera, focuses a situation that is after all less purely individual and more universal than is usually supposed.

So the contributions of Jean Sibelius to the theatre lay almost entirely in the domain of incidental music to plays, ancient or modern but mostly modern. And this leads to another circumstance. Incidental music for the theatre may be poetic, evocative, dramatic, elegiac; but it is seldom more than an adjunct to the play and usually minimized by being divorced from it, though of course suites made from incidental music are often most agreeable. But this sort of music is more made than inspired: it seldom causes the creative fur to fly. The exceptions are usually where they would be predicted: the leading example is Beethoven's music to Goethe's *Egmont,* especially the great overture.†

The theatre has always played a leading part in Scandinavian cultural life. If the Norwegian Ibsen and the Swedish Strindberg head the rota of international dramatists, the list behind them is long and honourable.

---

*Tchaikovsky once said that it took a heroic act of will not to write opera, and he was not that much of a hero. He was also not heroic enough to eschew writing nonsymphonic symphonies. Sibelius was heroic enough to write true symphonies and to avoid writing operas, lacking for whatever reason the full creative impulse.

†Beethoven's inbuilt and incurable habit of compressing the essence of a drama into a comprehensive dramatic overture rendered all other incidental music redundant. It usually rendered the ensuing drama redundant. That is why, Mahler notwithstanding, *Leonora* no.3 (or no.2) should never be played within earshot of *Fidelio.*

Sibelius contributed music to twelve theatrical productions, ranging from a single number or a song or two, to a full score of pieces. Nowadays of course orchestras in theatre pit are virtually nonexistent outside the opera house. Music in this category has been almost entirely diverted to the cinema and tends to be more ephemeral, being too intimately bound up with the continuity of the film to have independent existence.* But during the nineteenth century and the early part of the twentieth there were widespread opportunities for music with plays all over Europe and America. There were also theatre occasions other than the production of plays that gave composers the chance of contributing—galas, celebrations, recitations, melodramas,† and historical pageants. Sibelius in the early years of his career took part in these—the ubiquitous *Finlandia,* as we have seen, came from one of them. No doubt many of this type of entertainment took place as much in the concert hall as in the theatre; but the principle holds.

Sibelius's theatre music is variable in quality, but the best of it is unmistakably from his hand and of fine distinction. Even at its weakest it is seldom anonymous, as his salon pieces frequently are. His first incursion into the theatre proper was in 1898 when he provided a quite substantial score to Adolf Paul's *King Christian II.* The play tells the story of how Christian, ruler of Denmark, Norway, and Sweden, falls in love with the low-born Dutch girl Dyveke, who is eventually murdured. The music (only four numbers appeared with the première; the rest were added later) is pleasant, apt, mildly Sibelian, in a popular Scandinavian style. It long outlived the play, which soon disappeared, and is still performed. The "Musette," which Sibelius said should ideally be for "bagpipes and reeds," is delightful; the "Elegy" agreeable in a Griegish manner; the "Nocturne" fairly extended but not all that memorable; the "Serenade" likewise. The rest is reasonably forgettable. But if *King Christian* is not prime Sibelius, even prime theatre Sibelius, it has its historical importance, for it was one of the first Sibelius scores to win a widespread and long-lived popularity outside Finland.

However, his next work for the theatre, music for *Kuolema* by his brother-in-law, gave rise to a piece which carried his fame far beyond anything dreamed of in the wake of the success of *King Christian.* The music for *Kuolema* consisted of six numbers for strings and percussion. The original score remains unpublished; but Sibelius rewrote the first number of it as *Valse triste,* a piece which, like *Finlandia,* carried his name far and wide through the world and made it familiar (and beloved) among those

---

*On the evidence of what he wrote for the theatre, it is clear that Sibelius, had he so wished, could have made a notable contribution to the cinema. It is, after all, only a kind of transference from one public medium to another.

†Like Elgar, Sibelius produced several examples of this curious form of entertainment between 1894 and 1925, seven in all. Most consist of instrumental accompaniments to recitations of verses by contemporary poets.

who would not contemplate sitting through a symphony by Sibelius (or by anyone else). *Valse triste* is a typical piece of popular Sibelius, with typical faults and virtues; it represents a prime example of the way the Sibelian idiom, at other times severe and uncompromising, could be turned easily to popular account, for like *Finlandia, Valse triste* has the authentic Sibelius tone and temper. These are not, like his salon pieces, merely agreeable and competent but lacking in any hint of individuality.

Rarer and more fetching is the way in which Sibelius brought together the third and fourth scenes from the play and turned them into a subtle and beautiful invocation known as *Scene with Cranes,* * by adding two clarinets to the original strings and percussion. It is an example of the other side of Sibelius: tender, gentle, suggestively poetic.

Probably the best known of Sibelius contributions to the theatre is the music he wrote for a production in Helsinki's Swedish Theatre of Maurice Maeterlinck's *Pelléas et Mélisande* in 1905. Maeterlinck's strange, dark-hued, symbolistic play has inspired more musical compositions than any other in the past hundred years, from Debussy's masterpiece of opera and Schoenberg's large, complex, post-Wagnerian tone poem, through incidental music by Sibelius and Gabriel Fauré. Sibelius made a concert suite out of his original score, consisting of nine numbers. If he did not penetrate the elusive essence of Maeterlinck's psychological drama as successfully as the two Frenchmen, Debussy and Fauré in their different ways did, several of the items reveal an individual response and demonstrate his working methods in this kind of activity. The whole score has been given an extra lunge of popularity through the use of one of its numbers, "At the Castle Gate" as the theme music for BBC television's long-running series, *The Sky at Night*. It is by no means the best excerpt from the suite, but it has no doubt encouraged many who would not otherwise have taken the trouble to explore further. The beautiful "Pastorale" with woodwind against ostinato strings, "Mélisande at the Spinning-Wheel," with its viola trills evoking the turning wheel and the rhythmic irregularities suggesting its offbeat movements, the light and shade of the "Ent'acte," and the imaginative use of string effects—chromatic harmonies, *sul ponticello* tremolos on the basses and high harmonics—in "By the Seashore," are excellent Sibelius in his lighter but not inconsequential vein. Taken as a whole, the *Pelléas et Mélisande* score might not establish Sibelius as one of the great composers; but it marks him out as an unusually accomplished one with a distinctive northern tone of voice.†

The next theatre score, for Hjalmar Procopé's pseudo-oriental play about unsavoury goings-on at the court of Babylon, is something different.

---

*It is recorded on the fourth side of Berglund's set of *Kullervo,* along with four items from *Swanwhite*.

†No one has evoked the inner poetic quality with so magical a touch as Sir Thomas Beecham.

Composers who address themselves to writing music for plays sometimes produce work that contains elements which are tangental, so to say, to their normal style and habits. Delius's splendid score for James Elroy Flecker's *Hassan* has passages that even hint at the influence of Stravinsky, unthinkable in the familiar Delian context and aesthetic; and in the music for *Belshazzar's Feast* Sibelius permits himself to dabble with something that sounds curiously like "Eastern Promise."* This is somewhat blatantly obvious in the "Oriental Procession," less obvious in "Khadra's Dance" (the full score runs to eight numbers; the concert suite has four); but it tends to infuse the whole, not perhaps surprisingly in view of the subject. Yet as with the Delius, it remains obstinately and unmistakably by its composer. "Khadra's Dance" even has a slither of *Valse triste* slipped into it and its sinuous oboe tune has a little triplet tag which is pure Sibelius. The two middle numbers, "Solitude" and "Night Music"—the first with solo viola and solo cello, the second with one of Sibelius's asymmetrical melodies for flute briefly reminiscent of *The Swan of Tuonela*—are effective and atmospheric. The flute is also to the fore in "Khadra's Dance," and the writing for bass clarinet is typical too.

Unlike *Pelléas et Mélisande* which is a permanent piece of theatre, *Belshazzar's Feast* permanently disappeared after a few initial performances. Not so Strindberg's *Swanwhite,* a play by a major writer which, even if it is not frequently produced, remains significant. So, in some of its parts, is Sibelius's music. Originally in fourteen "scenes," the usual concert suite was extracted from it, consisting of seven numbers. Of these the second, "The Harp," shows clear anticipations of the middle movement of the Fifth Symphony; the third, "Maidens with Roses," has much charm and some originality, and the fourth "Listen! The Robin Sings" is a delicate and highly poetic evocation (especially when sensitively played). Both "The Prince Alone" and "Swanwhite and the Prince" contain typically Sibelian elements of construction and expression, both terseness of musical ideas and modal inflexion of melody and harmony. Only the opening and closing numbers of the suite, "The Peacock" and "Hymn of Praise," are in the nature of somewhat empty gestures.

Between 1909 and 1916 Sibelius wrote four more sets of incidental music for the theatre. The most important of these appears to have been for Hofmannsthal's *Jedermann,* or *Everyman,* by which Sibelius himself set some store, though it is seldom heard and is, like so much of its kind, by no means consistent in quality. The score for Paul Knudsen's *Scaramouche* (1913) is quite copious, but again uneven and ultimately not all that impressive.

---

*Kajanus's outstanding recording from 1932 is included in one of the World Records albums containing the First and Second symphonies. A later stereo recording by Rozhdestvensky coupled with an alternative version of the Violin Concerto by David Oistrakh on HMV Melodiya is currently out of circulation (ASD2407).

To say that the music for Shakespeare's *The Tempest* is uneven and unimpressive is both true and misleading. In one sense, it represents a compendium of Sibelius's style and method in writing for the theatre: at its best entirely characteristic, and the finest of his writing for the genre; at its worst somewhat trite and obvious, though in both cases the tone is so obviously Sibelius that even a couple of bars would establish its authorship beyond question. *The Tempest,* like many of Shakespeare's plays, contains plentiful explicit opportunities for music; but Sibelius went further and provided even more: thirty-four numbers in all, for solo voices, mixed choir, harmonium and orchestra, broken down for concert performance into a Prelude and Two Suites.

The disparity of inspiration and invention throughout this ambitious score is probably an inevitable concomitant of the genre. Some passages in any play demand musical commentary that is truly incidental whereas others need a pressurized matching, so to say, between dramatist and composer. Therefore, in passing critical judgment on any such score, to make too much of an issue of the weak or 'made up' sections is neither helpful nor in the end aesthetically relevant. The task of writing incidental music as a genuine adjunct to stage dramas demands as much sheer technical ingenuity as pressure of creative imagination, frequently more. And in this respect Sibelius's music for *The Tempest* succeeds admirably. If Beethoven's *Egmont* music and Mendelssohn's for *A Midsummer Night's Dream* appear to constitute exceptions from opposite ends, they do not prove the rule but simply disobey it, thereby showing once again that in truly creative work there are no rigid rules. Beethoven said that he wrote the *Egmont* music "for love of the poet" (Goethe); in fact he wrote it for love of liberty, his imagination fired as so often by a fierce addiction to all themes of resistance to political oppression and the struggle for freedom, partly innate, partly inherited from the ideals of the French Revolution; while the particular poetic atmosphere of *A Midsummer Night's Dream* touched a specific nerve in Mendelssohn's creative faculty, maintained over the seventeen-year interval that separated the incidental music from the overture.

The Prelude to *The Tempest* in its full version (at its reappearance it is truncated) is an authentic Sibelius nature tone poem in miniature (not a symphonic poem for it contains little in the way of development). It is certainly onomatopoeic, though that is nothing new in Sibelius. To say, as has been claimed, that it is the most onomatopoeic piece ever written is a clear exaggeration: there have been plenty of onomatopoeic pieces at least since the seventeenth century. But it is undoubtedly a powerful and effective piece of storm music, entirely suited to its purpose. The extraordinary simplicity of its means is further evidence of Sibelius's absolutely assured technical skill at the end of his active career. Although it has little of the tension and terror of *Tapiola,* it still has a genuinely Sibelian exteriorized chill and ominous energy.

The rest of the music that makes up the two suites is a mixture of exquisite miniatures and reach-me-down "filler" pieces. If the latter seems too strong a term, it is so only in relation to the quality of Sibelius's music at its finest and most originally conceived and executed. Sibelius is by no means the only composer to write music that has all the evidence of his skill but little of his true personality. T. S. Eliot,* writing about W. B. Yeats, drew a distinction between poems which, though beautiful, "are only craftsman's work, because one does not feel present in them the particularity which must provide the material for the general truth." Eliot was speaking of Yeats's early poetry and in the process of demonstrating how the poet developed to command of the "general truth" by which he became a great and major writer. Comparisons between one art and another tend to be dangerous and misleading; but there are truths and principles common to both and which shed light both ways. The fact is that even after a poet or composer has achieved that freedom of speech and command of the general truth of which Eliot spoke, he will often produce what is no more than craftsman's work; work, that is, out of his workshop rather than his creative passion. Sibelius in particular frequently did precisely that, after he had achieved his personal free speech and penetration of general truth which probably first came to him complete in the Fourth Symphony, though of course it had come partially in several compositions prior to that masterpiece. And this "craftsman's work" is not, in this sense, merely that type of totally anonymous salon music that has so distressed his admirers and fuelled the scorn of his detractors: it comprises some very fine and characteristic examples of his art.

It is not surprising that most of his theatre music is craftsman's work; yet at its best the speech itself is often free and authentic. On the other hand, there are layers of quality within the category of craftsmanship. If the Sixth and Seventh symphonies and *Tapiola* achieve that ultimate transpersonal objectivity which is also the ultimate in the suprapersonal, the music for *The Tempest* reaches, in Sibelian terms, somewhere near the ultimate in craftsman's work.

It cannot be said that in all respects the music for *The Tempest* reveals Sibelius as wholly at one with Shakespeare; or rather let us say that he tended to see Shakespeare's play from his own point of view rather than Shakespeare's—always a danger in such circumstances, especially when translation from one language into another is concerned. But numbers like "The Oak-tree" and the "Chorus of Winds" are informed with a quality of imagination which raises craftsmanship to poetic heights and fills it with an additional quality of awareness.

The music is not of course all on the same level; some items, usually referred to as pattern music, are certainly not worthless, but do lack this

---

Yeats. First annual Yeats Lecture delivered to Friends of the Irish Academy at the Abbey Theatre, Dublin, 1940.

touch of liberating imagination, just as the works of certain eighteenth-century minor composers use the bone-structure of sonata form, such as it was,* without developing an informing creative response.

Whether the *Scènes historiques,* or indeed any of the music written for national or historic occasions, or tableaux, belong properly in the category of theatre or concert music, need not detain us for long. In any case, virtually all the theatre music survives in the extracted suites, so that for practical purposes it is all concert music.

The two sets of *Scènes historiques* rank among what is best described as Sibelius's intermediate music; that is to say, it inhabits a region between the symphonies and the best of the symphonic poems and the outright pattern or craftsman's work. Although the two sets are separated by more than a dozen years and a score of opus numbers, the internal evidence suggests that they belong to a joint creative impulse in Sibelius's mind. This is reinforced by the way in which the first set, originally produced in 1899, was revised in 1911, within shooting distance of the second set (1913-14). The best of the *Scènes historiques,* like the best of the theatre music proper, is first rate entertainment music, clearly stamped with its authorship but lacking the quality of total genius that holds the attention even when it does not necessarily want to be held. The third number in the first set entitled "Festivo" in *Tempo di bolero,* is an apparent oddity although there are two other examples in Sibelius's work. The additions of castanets and some rather obvious recourse to the beat of the bolero does not alter the Sibelian perspectives. It is not perhaps quite a bolero on ice; but it is something not so far off—and that is an even greater oddity and more wilful paradox. The *Scènes historiques* contain better and worse music than "Festivo," and much of it is characteristic, identifiable at a glance or hearing; but at no point does it touch the pinnacle of the symphonies or the tone poems. It can, like much of the theatre music, be best taken as a good example of prime second-cut Sibelius.

*See "Conclusions".

5 : *Other Music*

Under this heading come two familiar large scale works—the Violin Concerto and the string quartet, *Voces intimae*—a certain amount of choral music including *Kullervo,* the rest mostly patriotic occasional work but containing a few worthwhile pieces; a quantity of songs—a fair number of high quality; and a disconcertingly long list of miscellaneous instrumental music, most of it strikingly nondescript. It is this latter category, the apparently endless stream of anonymous trivia he churned out virtually throughout his active career, which has most alarmed Sibelius's admirers and provided ammunition for his detractors. The volume of these compositions resulted, to some extent, from his urgent need of money. Indeed, there is no moral imperative which enjoins a man not to use his talent apart from his genius to turn an honest purseful. What is less artistically innocent is the way in which he seems actually to have liked the stuff and at various times to have written it for his pleasure as much as for his need. But that is another story; it will be confronted later.

The Violin Concerto, Sibelius's only major work for solo instrument and orchestra, has many characteristic features but ultimately it does not add up to a thorough-going Sibelian creation. Or rather, it convinces that it is by Sibelius, but abides a number of questions about the totality of his art that the best of the symphonies and symphonic poems do not. In the Concerto, the popular and the tough Sibelius meet, try to fuse, but end by remaining rather obstinately apart. At the heart of the work is a dichotomy of elements that will not lie down together. A certain dichotomy is in the nature of the concerto form (the word is from the Latin *concertare,* "to compete"); but that is not quite the matter in question here.

One of the conflicting elements is that of virtuoso effectiveness. Despite the external evidence, Sibelius was not primarily a virtuoso composer. His technique was assured and comprehensive: it could be turned to virtually any purpose. But it was not at bottom a technique that veered naturally towards display and the quick return. Yet the Violin Concerto is in more than one sense a compensation for, or sublimation of, Sibelius's unfulfilled ambition to become a virtuoso international violinist. Thus the display element is somewhat laid on, deliberately and by no means ineffectually. All the same, it does not lie easily beside his natural and endemic compositional style.

One would hardly deduce this from the opening pages, which are both masterly and masterful.* The principal theme soars, over *divisi* strings tremolo

and the continuation develops several typical Sibelian fingerprints. The intervalic structure of the fully evolved theme is characteristic; the "motor rhythm" inaugurated by the soloist at cue 4 throws a rope looping forward, and the juxtaposition of the lyric and the dramatic, most notably when confirmed by the orchestra, sets the overal tone of a composition that could hardly have originated from any other hand. The form too is original and typical in the way it alternates two contrasting groups of themes rather than directly developing either. Devices of the solo cadenza (written out) and augmentation take the place of the familiar Sibelian organic growth; yet the totality of the structure more than once hints at it. The trouble is not so much that the thematic material itself

---

*Heifetz is incomparable here. The tension and intensity of his playing puts all others in the shade: a unique achievement. David Oistrakh, Kyung-Wha Chung, and Isaac Stern are admirable; but Heifetz is in a class apart, both in his historic Sibelius Society recording with Beecham, and in the later RCA stereo, the latter a less masterful accompaniment but a superior recording.

and its working out does not cohere as that the aesthetic foundations are flawed. Music of overt display and Sibelius's powerful constructional principles make uncongenial bedfellows. Brahms in his Violin Concerto, and still more in the B flat Piano Concerto, had already demonstrated how sturdy constructional principles can be satisfactorily welded with effective solo work; but Sibelius did not find a parellel solution. Undermined perhaps by a subconscious memory of his own frustrated ambitions to become an international virtuoso of violin, he contrived a solo part which, though bristling with extreme, and legitimate difficulties for the soloist, frequently sounds like the display work of Vieuxtemps, or Wieniawski, or Sarasate and consorts ill with his characteristically tough and hardgrained way with the orchestra. The first-rate opening pages promise more than they can deliver. This is not in itself in any sense unique: several famous and enduringly popular compositions—Mendelssohn's *Italian* Symphony is a classic example—begin with memorable ideas that are not subsequently maintained. With Sibelius it is unusual because in virtually every important work the unity of the material is established at the outset and the structural cohesion integral to the musical thinking.

The slow movement pinpoints another questionable facet. It is lyrical, it is indulgent, it is genial. There is plenty of lyrical music in Sibelius, but it is at its best and most characteristic neither indulgent, nor genial, certainly never sentimental. This Adagio di molto in B flat, is decidedly sentimental; it is soft-centered; it does not ring quite true; and when it is badly played, its softness and emotionalism too easily and self-consciously indulged, it can be intolerable.* Despite many individual touches in the scoring and the thematic structure (the relationship of the main theme to the opening of the first movement for example), it is difficult to resist the idea that not only here but in the work as a whole, Sibelius strayed momentarily into creative fields not his own. It makes one wonder what manner of composer Sibelius would have become if he had allowed himself to be more or less permanently seduced away from the stern necessity that was to wring from him the uncompromising severity of the Fourth Symphony and *Tapiola*. That is the real nub of the matter. The geniality of the Violin Concerto is not the same as the comparative geniality of the Third Symphony where it is neither falsified by overemphasis nor grafted on from the outside. There is a note of nostalgia in this slow movement that is quite uncharacteristic of Sibelius; and that it is almost certainly a personal nostalgia for his own dream of becoming an international virtuoso rather than a more general late romantic yearning for some lost Eden that never was and never could be, does not alter the argument.

---

*Heifetz again is incomparable, desentimentalizing it as far as it will go.

Far from contradicting or challenging that proposition, the bustling finale with its impressive rota of violin pyrotechnics only confirms it. There is always an element of sentimental self-indulgence in overt display music. It is not always and necessarily the worse for that, provided it remains within its own orbit. But it is not a Sibelian orbit. This finale opens with some typical Sibelius "thrumming" rhythm which the soloist varies with the main theme:

The form is a kind of rondo; cross-rhythms are prominent. It does not add up to much, musically though it makes its effect, and the concerto as a whole is an attractive work, there is no denying that. However, Sibelius is out of his element.

When a composer of substance tries to apply his natural style to music that is by its nature insubstantial, the dichotomy is bound to show in ways by no means comfortable or congenial. It boils down to what Artur Schnabel used to say about only being interested in music that is better than it can be played. A great deal of music is only justified by brilliance of performance; that is to say, it relies upon executant rather than creative values. Again, there is nothing intrinsically wrong in that. The trouble may arise, however, when substantial means are applied to insubstantial ends. Then the dichotomy wounds.

Among full scale violin concertos, that of Sibelius stands reasonably high. But then it is not a very exalted category. One each by Beethoven, Brahms, Tchaikovsky, Elgar and Mendelssohn, of differing styles and value, and the list shortens until we arrive at Bartók, Schoenberg, Berg, Stravinsky. Yet these are not specifically display pieces; they have the kind of musical substance to be found in symphonic or other similar species of composition. Display music welded to taut, nonindulgent musical thinking is one thing; display music divorced from musical thought or integrity is another. The Sibelius concerto comes dangerously near the latter.

The string quartet, *Voces intimae,* raises some of the same questions, plus a few more, but for different reasons. There is nothing of over self-indulgence about the quartet, and very little of display, at least not beyond the accomplished artist's natural enjoyment in relishing his accomplishments.

In his youth Sibelius composed much chamber music, mostly prentice work, and what has survived is uncharacteristic and seldom heard.
But it served his purpose well for when he was engaged in putting the
cement into the foundations of his technique, he concentrated his exercise almost entirely into that form of composition. It was a discipline that
was to establish his unshakable technical equipment before he found his
proper medium with the orchestra.

Why Sibelius wrote no other serious chamber work except the string
quartet is as idle a question as why he wrote nothing at all after 1926. If he
had composed more chamber music during his active years, or more
pertinently, had turned to it, especially to the string quartet, as Beethoven
did, after his orchestral odyssey was over, who knows what alternative bias
might have been put on his total catalogue.

The quartet is Sibelian at a hearing. It is in some respects an amalgam
of Sibelius's mid-career style. It was written in 1909, between the Third
and Fourth symphonies; but its musical infrastructure reaches out also to
aspects of the Sixth and Seventh. It is in five movements, with two scherzi,
or movements of a scherzo character. The material does not parallel that of
the Seventh Symphony in any significant way, yet there are sufficient
internal linkages and cross-references to encourage the idea that somewhere in the Sibelian unconscious the one-movement form was taking
shape. The first movement, is clearly outlined, economical, lean-textured
and pivoting viably between tonality (D minor) and modal (Dorian), with
the feel of modality prominent throughout. If the opening theme comes
from the same creative regions as *Rakastava,* the movement soon settles
into a kind of "motor" figure that anticipates the Fifth Symphony. Indeed,
the most direct reference is to the Fifth, both in the internal motivations of
the outer movements and the apparent, but partially deceptive, innocence
of the slow one, another Adagio di molto.

A glance at a page or two of score, from any movement but especially
the first, might suggest the Sixth Symphony as well as *Rakastava.* But in
fact the impression is misleading. The quartet does not exactly parallel any
other composition of Sibelius; it stands on its own, stylistically as well as
physically, even if the majority of its pages are unmistakably by this
composer and no other. And that in itself is a kind of compliment, for it
does not intimate, necessarily, that it is above or below par, either
aesthetically or technically, simply that it is well written for its medium.
String quartets that look like orchestral music are common enough,
especially from composers who have a particular mastery of the
orchestra—and they are not good string quartets, any more than are those
which tend to look as though they have been transcribed from ideas
primarily devised upon, if not actually intended for, the piano. *Voces
intimae,* though it does not give the impression of overall concentration and
the absolute motivic unity of the later symphonies, the best of the
symphonic poems is nevertheless a true strong quartet, a true work of Jean

Sibelius. It has, presumably because it is in five instead of the more usual four movements, been likened to a kind of suite rather than a typically Sibelian organic growth.* That is going too far: it may not have the tight, inseparable logic throughout that is Sibelius's particular contribution to musical thinking, but it still has its own order of motivic unity and thematic integration. All the material derives from a common scalic source motif, remembering that musical motifs are always dynamic rather than static; that is to say, they will alter in specific shape and relativity without changing their essence or their origin. This, of course, is true of all Sibelius's musical practice and precept where the mutation of motifs is the generating principle of his symphonic structures: it is also true of the material of the string quartet, even if it is less rigorously held and maintained than in the Sixth and Seventh symphonies and *Tapiola*. And it hardly needs stressing that such motifs are harmonic and rhythmic as well as thematic.

The solitary string quartet of Sibelius may open up more potentialities than it appears at first sight to fulfil; but it remains a valued and valuable item in his catalogue.

Although *Voces intimae* and the Violin Concerto are Sibelius's two major works outside the symphonies and symphonic poems, he did compose some other works on a lesser scale in both categories. Most of his other chamber music is early prentice work, seldom performed and not characteristic: it contributes little or nothing to our understanding of him and nothing at all to his reputation, one way or the other. On the other hand, he did write a number of smaller works in concerto form (all for violin) of considerable quality; the two Serenades Op.69, and the six Humoresques Opp.87 and 89. At first sight these might be seen to stand in much the same relationship to the Sibelius Violin Concerto as Beethoven's two Romances stand to his. In fact the demarcation is not quite so clear: the Beethoven Romances are obvious minor appendages to his concerto, which is an unchallenged masterpiece; but several of Sibelius's smaller pieces are superior and more consistent than the concerto, which is not entirely a masterpiece and certainly not unchallenged. The Serenades, dating from 1912/13, require a fairly large orchestra; brief though they are, they are characteristic of Sibelius, tone and technique. If a good deal of Sibelius's "minor" music is too minor to be worth bothering with, it is not on account of physical dimension. He could always deploy his vast technical accomplishment as well as his emotional and intellectual attributes on a small scale as readily as on a large one. Nor was his music of this

---

*Perhaps the existence of an early (1889) string trio in five-movement suite form influenced certain unconsidered judgments on the quartet, even though the trio is in conventional suite form, with dance measures as well as more formal ones, whereas the quartet is quite differently constituted.

description simply a case of "big" music unnaturally restricted: it was at its best genuine music on a small scale. The two Serenades are useful examples of this and so in a slightly different way are the Humoresques.

The Humoresques were written in 1917, when the First World War was at its crux and seemed as though it might never end, and also between the second and final versions of the Fifth Symphony. It was a lean time for Sibelius in every way. His mind may have been occupied with the problems of recomposing the Symphony; but social and political conditions did not encourage composition of any creatively significant kind, with civil war and deprivation and acute danger on all sides. Whatever the reason, Sibelius wrote nothing of importance apart from the Humoresques before the Sixth Symphony which appeared in 1923, though the nature and quality of the Sixth Symphony suggest that the years had only been fallow on the surface.

And perhaps some of the technical problems encompassed by the recomposition of the Fifth and the growth of the Sixth were reviewed if not finally solved in the varied nature and technical devices of the Humoresques. Perhaps too Sibelius's old regrets at not becoming a concert violinist rose again to the top of his mind, and in working them over he erected a small bulwark against the trials and hardships of the period. Either way, the writing for the violin is both virtuoso in the best sense and highly expert, by no means empty or merely rhetorical. Both numbers of Op.87 (b)* have what at first sight appear to be strong modal leanings but are in fact typical of Sibelius's harmonic procedures. They are modal, yes, but more in line with his usual practice almost from the beginning than due to any "influence," nevertheless they pitch forward in the direction of the Sixth and Seventh symphonies.† And the first of Op.89 (or No.3 in the conjunct sequence) with its orchestra of strings *divisi* only points the same way from a slightly altered angle.‡ Sibelius himself had a high opinion of the Humoresques, and he was not a man who invariably liked in hindsight everything that he had done or written. His own words in reference to them—"Life's sorrows and shafts of sunshine"—suggest that they probably had particular personal associations for him, whether purely private or both private and public.

Sibelius wrote a fair amount of choral music, much of it overtly patriotic and determinedly occasional, and in consequence seldom heard. At its head stands *Kullervo,* that early large-scale choral/orchestral work with which he made his first reputation but which he would not revise and

---

*The six Humoresques are often numbered consequentively 1-6, encompassing both opus numbers, 87 and 89.

†As we have seen in discussing the symphonies, modal devices were a typical feature of Sibelius's harmonic and melodic structures from the beginning. His attraction to the music of Palestrina which is supposed to have influenced the Sixth Symphony only served to emphasize and confirm it.

‡From the angle, originally, of *Rakastava.*

would permit no performance after the première during his lifetime. Yet *Kullervo* remains his most substantial and most important composition in this general category. It is not a masterpiece; but it is a remarkable work for a young man yet to establish a reputation and without experience of composing on a large scale. Though derivative in parts (inevitably in the circumstances,) it has that unique tone of voice which Sibelius alone extracted from chorus and orchestra.

The subject matter is derived from Runos XXXII and XXXIV of the *Kalevala* and deals with the exploits and misfortunes of the hero Kullervo, one of the legendary figures of Finnish mythology. In one sense the subject is neo-Wagnerian, though the actual musical idiom is far from that (if it is near anything, it touches here and there echoes of Tchaikovsky and the Russians, but even there not very much). During the course of his adventures, Kullervo encounters a beauteous maiden, entices her to accompany him on his travels, seduces her, and then discovers she is his lost sister. The rest of the story is quite un-Wagnerian, for the alarming discovery leads to the girl's immediate death and causes Kullervo, after desperately seeking death in battle, to throw himself upon his own sword and so end the intolerable misery. Wagner of course would have had none of that. In *The Ring* incest, far from being the subject of horror and despair, is seen as a dynamic, energizing principle: Siegmund and Sieglinde; Siegfried and Brünnhilde—the begetting of the new race of god-men depends both in the first and last places upon incestuous relationships. What is strange is that objection to (or horror of) incest belongs to civilized not to primitive societies, and therefore since both Wagner and Sibelius went back to saga and Norse mythology one would predict the reactions to be similar. Whereas Wotan tries to outwit and outargue Fricka over the Sieglinde-Siegmund incest, from which the hero Siegfried is born, a similar discovery by Kullervo and his sister leads to the opposite result; mutual death and dishonour.

The music of *Kullervo* anticipates the mature Sibelius at several points. The journeyings of Kullervo use the trochaic metre later developed with much effect for *Lemminkäinen's Return* and *Nightride and Sunrise;* there are several examples of Sibelius's gift for dark-hued melody; and the writing for voices, though often unsure, has a tone and texture only Sibelius could have built on. The scoring too is often characteristic. But beyond all this it is the power and scope of imagination that sets *Kullervo* down as a work of true genesis for the young composer. Much tightening, paring, refining, and purifying was required before the authentic Sibelius style and aesthetic could emerge from the chrysalis; but the creative pressure is there and cannot be mistaken.

For the rest, probably the only choral work worth consideration is *The Origin of Fire (Tulen synty)* also known as *Ukko the Firemaker,* for baritone solo, male voice choir, and orchestra, written for the opening of the Helsinki National Theatre in 1902. It is another piece drawn from the

Kalevala, and although reasonably good Sibelius music, has none of the originality or imagination of *Luonnotar.* It stands at the head of those innumerable occasional pieces Sibelius turned out from his workbench, more or less to order and frequently for public celebrations and national presitigious events. It is clear that Sibelius wrote easily and competently for massed voices; but they seldom inspired him. Most of his works in this genre fall into line with similar productions of Brahms of the order of the *Fest und Gedenksprüche* Op.109.

The solo songs are another matter. Sibelius may not have been one of the great and original songwriters; but the best of his songs reach a high standard and display aspects of his genius in a particular form and manner. The best of them are (predictably) nature pieces; but there are some also which deal convincingly with human emotions. His choice of texts was reasonably judicious, if not remarkable. He was a man of wide general culture, and considerable literary erudition, but his taste when it came to songwriting was not impeccable. And of course there is no absolute reason why it should have been. Schubert, prince of song-writers, had virtually no taste in literary matters and frequently made great songs out of feeble verse. Indeed, it might be argued that too fastidious a literary taste does not make for the best songs, if only because great lyric poetry tends to be complete in itself and the addition of music can add very little, if anything to it. Hugo Wolf's work may offer a contradiction to this argument; but even this is only partial.

Sibelius, however, had to face two problems unknown to the masters of the German *Lied:* those of melodic derivation and language. The German *Lied* had its origins in folk song and frequently embraced elements of both *Volkslied* and artsong; and even if the original language of the text was not German, a suitable translation could be made because of the musical hegemony of the German language. But for Sibelius it was different. Though Finnish folk song is clearly delineated within a restricted orbit, it was never subjected to that long process of evolution and extension which led to the flowering of the German *Lied.* Sibelius's songs therefore tend to be pure artsong; lacking a traditional seedbed they are sometimes artificial, even "arty," or else too self-consciously simple. And the language divisions tended to show, again because of the lack of any common, and commonly accepted, basic norm. He set Finnish, Swedish, and German texts, and each demands and requires a different tone and inflexion. Add to these his lack of total command of the piano, and his finest achievements in the realm of solo song are somewhat more remarkable than his failures*. Overall they may lack the inspired directness of

---

*Sibelius composed songs virtually throughout his career. His Op.1 is a set of five "Christmas Songs." Though by no means his earliest released compositions, these songs were given the primary opus number, by himself, in his own catalogue made in 1915. They appear to have been written between 1895 and 1913. For a long time little was known about them and they were not collated

Schubert's, the subtle sophistication of Wolf's or the almost frightening naturalism of Mussorgsky's, yet the best of them have an individual stamp hardly less notable than certain tone poems, the best of his theatre music, and some small scale orchestral scores like the Humoresques. On the other hand, not one has the sheer power and originality of *Luonnotar,* unquestionably his masterpiece of song, whatever category it may ultimately be argued to occupy. (*Luonnotar* is of course an orchestral song. Many of the songs with piano have been orchestrated; oddly, in view of Sibelius's frequently unexceptional accompaniments, not particularly to their advantage.)

But if none of the solo songs touches the total mastery of *Luonnotar,* the best have similar characteristics of melodic line and harmonic individuality. Among these are *Höstkväll* ("Autumn Evening," Op. 38 No. 1; *På verandan vid Hafvet* ("On a Balcony by the Sea,") Op. 38 No. 2, both from a group of five songs written between 1902-4 and both *echt* Sibelius, though contrasted in mood and tone; *Jubal* Op. 35 No. 1, with its emphasis on the unaccompanied voice, and *Teodora* Op. 35 No. 2 (1907/8), a kind of neo-Gothic love song; *Till Frigga* ("To Frigga,") Op. 13 No. 6 (1892); *En Slända* ("A Dragonfly,") Op. 17 No. 5 (1894); *Langsamt som kvällskyn* ("Slow as the Colours,") Op. 61 No. 1 (1910), and *Fafäng önskan* ("Idle Wishes,") Op. 61 No. 7, plus some of the Shakespeare settings in Swedish translations.

A number of Sibelius songs are handicapped by his less than masterful way with the piano. His strong suit was his ability to project a sudden chord with a tangible relationship to some sensual evocation in the text or context; it is almost like the quick scent of a plant or other natural phenomenon which immediately conjures up a whole area of provoked emotion. His weakness is a tendency to meander through keyboard clichés or commonplace figurations and sequences. The prevalence of the latter often undermines an otherwise promising song; but the potentiality of the former can flash a sudden illumination or probe of reality into another.

Both propensities characterize his music for piano alone. He was not a pianist and he did not excell here any more than in the accompaniments to his songs; yet he wrote for the keyboard from 1893 through to 1929 (his last listed, though unpublished, composition is five *Esquisses* for piano Op. 114). The best of his solo piano music is in the early Sonata Op. 12, the three lyric pieces entitled *Kyllikki* Op. 41 (1904), and the three small but effective Sonatinas Op. 67 (1912). Even here however little of the real Sibelius emerged: it was simply not his metier—too much of his piano writing, both here and hereafter, is orchestral rather than genuinely pianistic

into a single edition. However, they were issued in a properly edited version together by Edition Frazer, Helsinki, in 1975 and internationally in 1979 (F.M. 06353-7). They were probably written for home consumption when Sibelius's family was young and children were about the house. Sibelius's songs as a whole have sometimes been called "underrated": they in fact represent a particular perspective of his genius from one narrow angle.

in origin. Most of it sounds like not too convincing transcriptions of sections from the tone poems or chippings from the early symphonies.

For the *Kyllikki* pieces Sibelius turned once again to his beloved *Kalevala,* and to another part of the Lemminkäinen legends therefrom. It concerns the determination of Lemminkäinen to win Killikki, one of the maidens of Saari, for his bride; how he carries her off and eventually makes a pact with her that he will forgo the pleasures and pursuits of war if she will swear never to return to her village. She breaks her vow, whereupon Lemminkäinen sets off to find recompense in battle and the wooing of the Maiden of the Northlands, Pohjola's Daughter. The music is atmospheric, evocative, and quite skilfully written, yet the impression remains that it would better have been distilled into an orchestral tone poem.

The sonatinas are perhaps a little more pianistically effective, but less poetically potent. They are probably his best piano pieces in that they are obviously music written for the keyboard, unlike the majority of Sibelius's other piano music which sounds as if it has strayed from some temporarily closed orchestral workshop.

But while the piano pieces are not always anonymous, that charge has to be levelled against the mass of salon pieces that bestrew his catalogue. Sibelius produced these pieces by listening in restaurants to salon music and then going home to write it. But it is not the triviality of his salon music that distresses—that was his business—but its total anonymity. It is well made, undoubtedly competent, often very pretty in the style of international salon music, heard all over the world where the European has settled. But it is still anonymous. When Beethoven wrote waltzes for a Vienna coachmen's ball, it still sounded like Beethoven, even if like Beethoven when he was thinking about something else; when Mozart wrote a Serenade for the marriage of burgomeister's daughter it sounded exactly like Mozart, even if, as Constant Lambert observed, he wrote it cynically to pay for the rent and a little champagne. Elgar's salon music is brushed by the breath of Edward Elgar. But with the salon music of Sibelius, that is different. He who could sign his name with a bar or two of divided strings, a turn of woodwind, a thrust of brass chording, left no hint or trace of his own hand on his salon pieces; that is why they have so damaged his reputation. They are neither under- nor over-rated; they are not in the context of Sibelius rateable at all. They are not bad; in fact many of them are rather good, of their kind. And that in the context is what more than anything make them thoroughly unnerving.

To argue that the gap between Sibelius's best and most truly creative music and his salon music is greater than with any composer of comparable stature is a commonplace of criticism. But in fact the gap is not a void: it is full of stepping stones. These consist of pieces of varying types and quality, orchestral, vocal, instrumental, and graded quality that lie scattered among the masterpieces and near-masterpieces from *Kullervo* to and past the Seventh Symphony and *Tapiola.* One cannot say that Sibelius was a creative schizophrenic, for his creative hand knew very well what his talented hand was doing—nevertheless he could keep the two apart to an unusual extent. It does not affect his stature one way or the other however; it can be observed but need no longer be made an issue. Chips off the block? Hardly. Chips from the communal pile more likely; gleanings from the beach when the tide is out to keep the fires burning—and that perhaps in a more profound sense than appears at first sight. It was probably necessary for him to work the trivial and the anonymous out of his system by music itself rather than by extraneous means, in order to clear the hearth for the creation of the wholly personal, wholly individual works, those in which the particular is transmuted into the general, the subjective into the transcendentally objective, in other words, that fusion of the subjective and the objective, the personal and the impersonal out of which all great art is finally made, and must be made.

6 : Conclusions

Sibelius once said to Bengt de Törne*: "When we see these granite rocks we know why we can treat the orchestra as we do." It was a revealing remark, though one that should cause no surprise. It is not only the overtly nationalist composer who is consciously affected by the nature of the environment, by landscape, and geophysical structure: it is an integral part of the total configuration of the individual as well as the collective consciousness. Landscape and temperament are closely interrelated; not only in composers; not only in artists of any kind; but in every sentient human being, wherever from, whatever the calling or vocation.

There are landscapes and landscapes; and there are rock strata and rock strata; each conditioning if not finally determining. Limestone is not the same as sandstone; chalk is not the same as dolomite; marble is not the same as granite. Even granite is not always the same: the reddish brown granite of Finland is not the same as the grey granite of Cornwall. For Sibelius the determination was not of course granite alone; the totality of the landscape and topography became, with history and social evolution

---

*Sibelius: A Close-Up

what went into the making of the man and artist, the realized personality. The sound of Sibelius, instantly recognizable but as always virtually impossible to analyse, derived from various ingredients, geographical, ethnic, national, most of all personal. His forms too emanated from a temperament directly conditioned by geography and ethnics, "that of soul and that of race."* It is all of a piece: it has to be, or the final artwork must be divided and ennervated.

Since Sibelius was primarily a composer of symphonies it is necessary before reaching for the final conclusion to offer some examination of symphonic form *per se*. There may be those who argue that no musical or artistic form exists *per se;* and in so far as symphonic form, sonnet form, cyclic form, narrative form, any other that may be named is, like every significant motif, dynamic not static, that is true. On the other hand, if there is no irremovable foundation, no form can in the end survive or contribute to that evolutionary process by which alone life and vitality can be maintained, period to period, generation to generation.

The principal characteristic of true symphonic thinking lies in continuity. And this is precisely where the romantic symphonists went astray—this and their determination to have the externals of sonata form clash with their basically discursive ideas and material. Despite their outward size the first movements of Beethoven's Third, Seventh and Ninth symphonies contain little extraneous or diversionary matter; and the first movement of the Fifth, while not exactly shortcircuitng conventional sonata form, is shorn of all the customary bridge work and transitional matter to produce an effect of intense concentration. The first movement of the Fourth Symphony, the Allegro molto vivace after the Quasi adagio introduction with its mysterious probings into the unconscious, stands nearer to the *Eroica* in style and technique but has also something of the purity of the Fifth. Beethoven was the supreme master of concentration of musical thought in the symphony. And not only in the symphony: in works like the first *Rasoumovsky* string quartet, the F minor Quartet, Op.95, several piano sonatas, the *Egmont* and *Leonora No.3* overtures the same basic process of creative concentration is in evidence.

After Beethoven the symphony proper could go in one of two directions: either it could become illustrative and discursive, and so lose its essential character; or it could progress in the direction of increasing complexity of form and organization. The romantics took it one way—the first—and were inevitably led into confusing symphony with tone poem and music drama of one kind or another. But until the maturity of Sibelius no one advanced it significantly in the second and more demanding direction. Tchaikovsky and Mahler composed symphonic autobiographies of varying kinds; Bruckner wrote huge canticles for orchestra; Dvořák created fresh-toned nature poems in four movements, though a partial

---

*W.B. Yeats *Under Ben Bulben*

exception may be made in the case of the D minor Symphony, which casts envious glances in the direction of Brahms. But only Sibelius took the problem of taut symphonic thinking, uncompromising and severely logical, a major step forward.

And in a sense this was inevitable. The classical symphonic form was the outcome and a rational reflection of a particular age and period, a specific social and intellectual environment. As Charles Rosen has argued, "sonata form could not be defined until it was dead. Czerny claimed with pride around 1840 that he was the first to describe it, but by then it was already part of history."* Most post-Beethoven symphonists either did not recognize that truth or did not know how to cope with it. Schubert had begun to work his way out of the dilemma, but he died too young; Wagner eschewed orchestral symphony†; Berlioz made a peace of his own; Liszt called a couple of works "symphony" but otherwise left the past decently interred. The tremendous evolutionary leap which followed the French Revolution, signalled the Romantic Revival and fed one side of the nineteenth century with material so combustible that only those with the strongest nerves could survive. It also shattered the older forms and stylistic procedures. Those who pretended that it had not, the "traditionalists," followed the usual course of anyone confronted with a rapid change which they cannot assimilate and who either turn to obstruction (like Hanslick) or try to argue their way out by a kind of what-was-good-enough-for-my-father tactic. Either way it would not work.

Nearly all the romantic symphonies are discursive, frequently picturesque. What is lacking is that sense of musical continuity and intellectual discipline which welds a true symphonic structure together. It is not that such music is unattractive, even without its own order of creative value: it is often both immensely attractive and of aesthetic value. But it still both evades and avoids the essential symphonic problem. There is of course no reason why music should not be discursive, illustrative, or picturesque, or all three at once. There is every reason why it should be—in the right context—but the symphony is not the right context. Orchestrally, some form of the tone poem is the appropriate medium for that sort of thing. It has been demonstrated in a previous chapter that Sibelius understood the difference when he made a clear distinction between symphony and symphonic tone poem. If his own tone poems are seldom vagrant or discursive to any marked extent, but tend to be tautly and logically constructed in the manner of the symphonies, it is simply because he had that type of musical mind. There is plenty of illustrative music in the Sibelius symphonic poems, some

*Charles Rosen, *The Classical Style* (London: Faber & Faber, 1971, 1976; New York, 1970)
†Apart from an early example, a Symphony in D (L832) showing exuberant youthful influences of Beethoven, Schubert and Weber.

picturesque touches; but the forms are stricter than with the more unabashed or brazen romantics.

The subjective romanticism of the period between the death of Beethoven and the maturing of Sibelius needed and compelled its fullest expression in music in new forms and fresh concepts. Many, led by Liszt, Wagner, Berlioz, Weber, Schubert at the beginning, by instinct rather than intellectual perspicacity or theoretical brainwork, did precisely that. But too many would lay their romantic feelings on the uncongenial bed of sonata form, or what they imagined to be sonata form, with its balanced periods and exact formal thematic and tonal oppositions (the characteristics of the classical age in fact). But more, it was at bottom a matter of direction, of the essential conjunction between form and feeling in any art at any time. As T. S. Eliot said of the sonnet of Shakespeare that it is not simply a particular rhyme pattern or scheme but a precise way of thinking and feeling, so the orchestral symphony is not a pattern of themes and keys and movements, but no less a precise way of thinking and feeling in music. And just as the sonnet, whether Shakespearean or Petrarchan, iambic blank verse, or the Spenserian stanza with the ottiva rima and the concluding Alexandrine, does not, and cannot, suit every poet, does not represent for him that particular conjunction of form and content out of which art is truly made, so symphony does not suit every composer. The trouble is that not all composers know it.

If that is so, then in the matter of true symphonic thinking we have to bypass virtually the whole of the nineteenth century. Among all the large-scale compositions labelled "symphony," with or without a qualifying adjective or subtitle, we search in vain for work that appears to grow spontaneously from its form instead of the form being imposed upon it. Only the four symphonies of Brahms constitute a real problem; and it is one that is still not satisfactorily solved or impartially reviewed. Brahms's supporters argue that if he does not rival Beethoven in symphonic power and scope, so be it—there are more ways than one of writing good symphonies (which is true). His detractors retort that although there are many different kinds of symphony, symphonic style still means something precise, even if it is not readily defineable (which is also true), and that by the most rigourous standards Brahms in his symphonies, despite noble effort, does not pass muster.

Brahms possessed a formidable sense of musical architecture and a very informed and assured technique, both essential to the composition of symphonies and he could handle form in the largest scale. All the same, it is doubtful if his mental processes moved naturally in terms of symphonic style, strictly so-called. For one thing, although he possessed a philosophic cast of mind, he did not possess a notably dramatic one; and drama is one important constituent part of symphonic form. In the First and Third symphonies he adopts the principle used by Beethoven of having two large outer movements flanking two small inner ones, thus making the specific gravity of three out of four: Sibelius also used a modification of this;* but Brahms, lacking the truly dramatic imagination, could not always match the "inners" with the density of his "outers." His finest work is to be found in his chamber music and his late piano pieces. His most notable effort in symphonic form is the finale of the Fourth Symphony; but that at bottom is only an adaptation, a technically superb one certainly, of an old established principle. Brahms's Passacaglia is a magnificent achievement; but as a contribution to the symphonic style it is neither here nor there, even though it is absolutely characteristic. †

Much the same, though on a more modest scale, may be said of Dvořák. Dvořák composed highly attractive music, put it into four movements, called it symphony and was not particular if it wandered about in the territory of symphonic tone poem. In the D minor (and to a lesser extent the D major) he came as near as his temperament and nature would allow to writing a symphony; but for the rest he wrote irresistible music full of originalities of harmony and tonality, charged with fluent melody, and anticipating at times the coming of atonality, though with no conscious or deliberate intent. But in the end Dvořák lapsed into the fanciful discursiveness of the *New World*. Even before that he had begun to backslide into the merely picturesque: the G major, though hardly symphonic in any recognizable sense, is his most characteristic, and most alarmingly attractive. His best orchestral music is in his tone poems and his best of all, like Brahms, in his chamber music. And that, opera or music drama apart, is the story of the nineteenth century and its musical romanticism.

Am I being pedantic? Very well then: I am being pedantic. But it is useful to make such distinctions and to underline the essentially symphonic nature of Sibelius's mind and creative faculty, not only for its own sake but because of its specific importance in understanding his individual consciousness and thus his importance as a central figure of the age and the period out of which we ourselves grew.

But what I am talking about in fact goes far beyond musical form and aesthetics considered in the abstract. It strikes directly into the human consciousness itself and the transformation of its structure in the light of continuing evolutionary progress. We speak, rightly, of the clash between classical forms and romantic feelings. But the real clash goes farther and deeper. It originates in the nature of the classical forms and style and the particular social and historical environment which created them. The classical sonata form and the classical symphony, while reconciling two apparently opposing dramatic concepts, are the outward expressions of the

---

*See p.78

†Although his earlier music shows occasional technical and stylistic derivations, or expansions from Brahms, there is, with Sibelius, no sense of nostalgic regret, or the irrevocable. The music of Sibelius honours the past, but belongs to the present and looks to the future.

finite and formal idea of man and his destiny, an idea which reached its highest and most developed point in the latter half of the eighteenth century. It was in effect an intelligent recognition of human limitation—which is one reason why many of the late romantics, and also W. B. Yeats, referred to it as the "hated century."

The great thrust of new knowledge and passionate energy, which was nominally initiated by the French Revolution, the huge evolutionary jump forward which tore the later nineteenth century assunder and created the modern age, was both the cause and the result of the romantic movement, or crisis. This new emergence transformed man's awareness of himself and his world from the finite to the infinite, from the static to the dynamic, from the formal to the existentially malleable. And it is precisely here that the dichotomy in the romantic symphony originates. It now becomes the outward expression not of a created order within recognized concepts, but of the internal quarrel in romantic man between the finite and the infinite, the fact of limitation and mortality and the existential sense of immortality and unlimited potential. The genius of Beethoven, coming as did at the pivot point, at the crux of the crisis, preserved an equable balance (though only just) largely by so recharging the classical finite that it could begin to contain the infinite. All the same, by the end of his life, and especially in the last quartets and sonatas, he had already moved out of the finite into the infinite, taking much in musical form and style with him, though it was not properly recognized for nearly a century.

The finiteness of the classical ideal does not of course preclude variety or scope of invention. It is in no sense rigid in the stultifying way of mere formalism. It is a philosophical and metaphysical idea that determines a total world- and life-view. Goethe, another pivotal figure, summed it up when he said that the master reveals his power through recognition of his limitations.

But that would not do for the romantics—at least not for the all-or-nothing romantics. Wagner was the archetype of the High Romantic; but he was not alone. He represented not only a generation but, as Thomas Mann argued, the entire nineteenth century. Wagner had strength of mind and character, as well as a certain shrewdness. Others were not so well endowed, and the romantic dream ultimately decimated itself in excessive introspection or went into the recklessly neomysticism of Scriabin's musical orbits.

The romantic ideal degenerated and collapsed, materially in war and revolution, musically in the corroborative excess of post-Wagnerian chromaticism. Beethoven had left the door open into the future; but although he was revered by the succeeding generations, the full import of his last works was not completely undersood, still less acted upon. Not that it mattered: music had to find new paths into a new world. It was not until the maturity of Sibelius that some of the threads, notably those relating to orchestral symphony, were picked up and projected into the future, and then only by an exercise of the most rigourous control—the kind of control that, perhaps by paradox, released once more the inner forces that had frustrated and hamstrung the romantics. There was gain and loss, as there had to be: the responses had got out of hand and it was necessary to reconstitute them.

The next logical step was the serial symphony, in which unity was based upon a new order and newly defined relationships. It was Schoenberg who saw the problem clearly and felt himself obliged to tackle it. Post-Wagner chromaticism, post-romanticism, had gone not only as far as it could go, but actually farther. From that point of view a radical transformation was required. But it was not the only point of view. Schoenberg's First Chamber Symphony and First String Quartet set the new course. Yet that order and that logic, though intellectually satisfying and emotionally potent, tended to be arbitrarily imposed by the serial technique which Schoenberg eventually created. Serial composition, though the vogue for some years, did not suit all composers any more than had previously sonata form or orchestral symphony. Though logical and in one sense inescapable, the serial symphony is in the highest degree artificial. It is based upon a form of that systematic determinism—instead of natural relationships—which returns the symphony to its former finiteness, and at its worst, it tends to that very rigid formalism, from which the romantics had striven to free it, even if they wrecked the vessel in the process. Technically, serialism gave back to the symphony the order of logical continuity it had lost when the romantics poured their existential quarrels into it; but at the same time it was in danger of losing that infinite flexibility and evolutionary responsiveness demanded by the emerging contemporary human consiousness.

The dichotomy remains, though in a slightly different form.

Sibelius was very far from being a serial composer in any accepted sense. On the other hand, only by stretching language beyond its accepted limits can he be called, in his later works at least (from the Fourth Symphony onwards that is) a "tonal" composer. There is a form of tonality in his music, and a form of modality; but as much as the music of Arnold Schoenberg, Alban Berg, and Anton Webern, it represents a drastic and radical modification of the tonal concepts of the classical era, in line with his drastic and radical modifications of form.

The parallel however is not with Schoenberg or any of the Second Viennese School, nor with any serialist, not with Stravinsky or the neoclassicists, but with Béla Bartók. In the context of the music of the first half of the twentieth century the seven symphonies of Sibelius stand in closest relationship to the six string quartets of Bartók. It is not that the Sibelius symphonies are in any significant sense like the quartets of Bartók: it is simply that the two series define the most potent and genuinely creative extension of the inner principles of sonata form, derived from Beethoven's late works; perhaps the only significant extension and development since the death of Beethoven.

Both series begin from romantic, nationally inflected origins—
Sibelius with the First Symphony (1899), Bartók the First Quartet
(1908)—and each ends with the respective composers evolving their subtlest and most advanced solution to their particular problem. In between,
the process of individual evolution progresses by differing means towards
the specific ends. Just as each symphony of Sibelius advances from one
point of view or another the growth and maturation of his symphonic
style, so the successive quartets of Bartók advance similarly. In each case
there is a clear case of growth, not only within each individual composition but within the series as a whole. Bartók's experiments with
form, particularly his use of "arch" form whereby in a five movement
scheme two pairs are closely related while the central fifth stands alone as
the apex of the arch, are not exactly paralleled in Sibelius. On the other
hand, both handled form, a derivation of classical form in a fairly loose
sense, in a manner calculated entirely towards achieving greater coher-
ence, greater motivic unity, greater organic growth by different means.
And if one argues that both Sibelius and Bartók moved progressively
from romanticism towards a form of classicism seems a trifle naïve, it still
contains a kernel of truth substantial enough to open a viable line of
discussion. If organic growth in Sibelius appears more nuclear, more a
matter of natural mutation of material, while Bartók's appears based
more upon the most skilful and discriminating use of technical devices,
that does not alter the submission or make the one "natural" and the
other "artificial." All works of art are a necessary mixture of the natural
and the artificial: they require inner vitality and organization propor-
tionately blended. Although Bartók frequently resorted to some kind of
cyclic form which bears no relation to Sibelius's precept or practice, the
objective remained the same: a greater integration and more organic
fusion of diverse elements. Indeed, Bartók in the Third Quartet attempts
formal integration by means of the concentration of his material into a
single continuous movement, while at the same time exchanging themes
and melodies for brief pregnant motifs capable of infinitely varied treatment and their own form of creative mutation.

What remains clear is that both Bartók and Sibelius worked by
different means towards similar ends, both beginning from the basis of
classical sonata form but achieving early on freedom from the irrelevancies
that ensnared most of the immediate predecessors and many of their
contemporaries. If sonata form could mean anything in the first half of the
twentieth century, it was Sibelius and Bartók who made it so. The
symphonies of Sibelius and the string quartets of Bartók stand as eternal
monuments to the power of tradition and the potentialities of the present
in a specific contemporary relationship.

But any achievement once it is complete has already become part of
the past. The avant-garde is always overtaken by its own momentum, is
always old fashioned the moment it has achieved any of its objectives.

Sibelius was never of the avant-garde, certainly not of that aspect of the musical evolution which was concerned with a radical transformation of the basic language. Yet he was in another sense truly prophetic,* though not in the sense promoted by his most devoted admirers during the 1930s. That is where Gray, Lambert, Olin Downes, and others who nailed their colours to his masthead went wrong: he did not show the way to the future. His achievement was complete in itself, as was Schoenberg's ultimately, and all attempts to found a school or flatter by imitation only confirmed once again Hemingway's truth that "the individual is all you ever have and all schools only serve to classify their members as failures."† It is always the same and it always was and will be. The Wagnerian school only showed that Wagner had exhausted his own ground; the Debussyistes did nothing but demonstrate the original quality of Debussy himself; in jazz the followers of Charlie Parker who sat around waiting for Parker's latest record to know what they should do next and were reduced to impotence after Parker's death were only wasting their time. It was the same with those who imagined they could get away with writing symphonies on the back of Sibelius's own original achievement: indeed the overpraise of Sibelius led to his subsequent downfall.

It is possible to argue that Beethoven had for the time being exhausted the potentiality of the symphony, in the sense in which Eliot argued that Virgil, or indeed any classic writer, exhausts the idiom and language so that it must lie fallow for some generations before its potential can be recovered.‡ Certainly the shade of Beethoven hung heavily over the symphonists who followed him. Brahms was eloquently conscious of the shade of the master looking over his shoulder; Schubert died with a vision of the dead Beethoven visiting his sickroom. No one was free from the omnipotent presence. Wagner saw the truth; saw that the legacy of Beethoven and the Ninth Symphony lay not in a continuation along those lines but rather in the new combination of voices and orchestra. This combination, which Beethoven had introduced was not an essential part of symphonic thinking but a fresh departure with as yet unexplored potential in the dramatic field.

Although many symphonies were composed after Beethoven, there was no significant advancement in true symphonic thinking until the end of the century when the full impact again became manifest.

Ironically, that manifestation only occurred in the works of two apparent opposites, with the hybrid symphony, as many still think the Beethoven Ninth to be, in Mahler, the pure symphonic style in Sibelius. But both in the deeper relationship derive from Beethoven.

---

*See p.72
†*Death in the Afternoon,* p.98
‡T. S. Eliot, *What Is A Classic?* (London: Faber & Faber)

Sibelius was a many-sided man. The more one tries to pigeon-hole him, the more elusive he becomes. Apparently something of an artistic monolith, Sibelius is far more multitextured than is revealed by a casual or even a conventionally close inspection. He has to be accepted on his own terms, taken at his own valuation in all his changing moods. He is by no means the most versatile of composers; yet his total output contains more variety than is often supposed. There is an idea too that the music of Sibelius contains little or no "ethical appeal"; and there is truth in it if, by ethical appeal, we mean the traditional humanistic attitudes. (Nor will everyone agree that works of art ought to have ethical appeal. That too is a legacy of Beethoven, and not necessarily a valid or encouraging one.)

We come nearest to clear thinking on this subject if we understand that for Sibelius, Nature, hostile and potentially destructive, has taken the place occupied by Fate in the Beethoven and post-Beethoven eras. It was all very well for Haydn, Beethoven, and Schubert to disport themselves in the woods and fields around Vienna, the friendly and congenial *Wienerwald,* and compose agreeable pastoral music in tranquility. And Vaughan Williams could ruminate on the undulating landscape of southern England and write his *Pastoral* Symphony, even if that was originally conceived in France and in the horrific conditions of the Western Front during World War I. Mahler too could tell us what the flowers said to him (as well as what the subjective demons also had to say). In the temperate regions even winter with its occasional minor hardships and discomforts is fundamentally little more than a time for skating and the throwing of snowballs. The ruddy-faced cheerfulness of a Dickensian Christmas is symbolic of domesticated winter.

But for the Finn, the dweller in far northern harshness where Nature as often as not strikes to kill even more decisively than in a Sutherland landscape at its most ominous, the situation is rather different. For him nature is seldom the scene of easeful repose and romantic consolations in gentle rusticity, ruffled by nothing more ominous than the occasional rowdy thunderstorm after which a Hymn of Thanksgiving may be gratefully sung. There Nature becomes the enemy, waging perpetual warfare against human endeavour and human aspiration, nearer in terms to the Vaughan Williams *Antartica* than to his own or Beethoven's *Pastoral*. But even in *Antartica* in the end the human spirit predominates, which it only does in Sibelius after the most resistant penetration and the most formidable struggle. In Finland, as in the far North in general, the elemental forces of nature can too easily be seen as a form of Fate knocking at the door all too insistently.

It is Sibelius's insight into the cold ferocity and antagonistic violence of Nature which gives his music its unique sound and its specifically modern significance. The history of man in nature is a long and intriguing one. Primitive man had a primitive terror of the natural forces—a terror from which he tried to escape by a process of personifying natural phenomena. Images of gods and animals became mixed up with images of man: human personality was in bondage to Nature and could only free itself by a long and laborious struggle. Later, the rise of humanism succeeded in elevating man to his position of primacy in the universe. Man emerged as free, autonomous, and independent personality. Only the blindly superstitious elements in organized religion threatened to drag him back. By the eighteenth century mankind thought it and its rationalism had prevailed. Nature was tamed, domesticated, and laid out in formal patterns for civilized pleasure. The more untamable and unregenerate aspects were looked upon with curiosity and held a kind of exotic charm; large mountains and wild places tended to be designated as "horrid"–simply another aspect of "charm." Natural disasters like the Lisbon earthquake, while causing general alarm, only served to make civilized man more than ever certain of his good fortune and his good sense. Contemporary reactions to the tragedies of the ancient world such as the destruction of Pompeii are illuminating. Nearly all of this, predictably, took place in the temperate regions of the European mainland.

Then came the nineteenth century with its romanticism and its rediscovery of natural demonism. The recipe now became the search for solace and a healing of the wound through oneness with nature. This in itself was no new idea; but it took a significantly different turn for the romantic generations. Man still held the centre of the stage, and personality was exalted. Fate or Destiny became personalized and could be tackled on the subjective plane. Individual and universal ills could be cured, or at least alleviated, by a return to nature. Paradise could be regained not only through communion with beasts, birds, and trees (*vide* Siegfried), but even more by some kind of mystical penetration to the spirit of the cosmos. But in the end that would not work either.

It would not work largely because of the enormous jump forward in accumulated knowledge and scientific revelation, the "knowledge explosion" as it has been called, foreshadowed in the eighteenth century, hammered out in the latter half of the nineteenth, but witheld in its full impact until the twentieth, which transformed the entire structure of human consciousness. Freud, Rutherford, Einstein–these and their like overturned the former ideas of human and animate nature with their concepts and discoveries. The stark hostility of natural forces came once more to a head. Science, which had appeared to give man independence of nature in the matter of subsistence and production, exposed a more potent form of dependence, even of a profound slavery to nature, that had never before been seen or understood. Freud unlocked the unconscious and revealed the full force of the primitive antagonisms and brutalities active yet. Two world wars underlined the scope of the avarice, prejudice, primeval cunning, and sheer elemental savagery barely concealed below the polished surfaces. The idea of the inevitability of progress seemed, at least on the human and natural level, forcibly suspended, to say no more.

In fact it was not so much a misconception as a misunderstanding of the true meaning of evolutionary progress. The splitting of the atom revealed the full power of latent destructiveness in nature. In a sense, man had come full circle. Optimistic belief in human potentiality and the supremacy of the human will suffered severe setbacks. Dependence on primitive nature, once thought to have been left behind for good, came roaring to the surface again. The innate hostility of nature emerged anew.

Wagner tried, true to the romantic tradition, to return man to nature. *The Ring* ends with the Rhine overflowing its banks and obliterating all trace of the previous squabbles and intrigues. The earth is young, fair, and a maiden again. Unfortunately, there is no reason why the whole sordid process should not begin over again, the entire cycle of wrangles, deceptions, arguings, and manipulations be repeated beginning to end, not once but *ad nauseam.* And therein lay the *cul de sac* of romanticism. Nature could do nothing but repeat itself: it was caught on the eternally spinning wheel of its own finiteness.

The dilemma for modern man was immense. It had to be faced on two planes: the confrontation face to face with the forces of hostile nature that reduce human potential and undermine his independence; and the use of science and technology to achieve dissociation from nature in the primary activities. Sibelius took the first course, the atonalists and serialists the second. The criticism that atonal and serial music runs against the grain of nature by ignoring, or actively flouting, natural relationships of sound misses the point.* Ostensibly, atonal and serial music came about in consequence of the dead end of post-Wagner chromaticism. But in fact it represented a recognition, partly conscious, partly unconscious, that science and technology were progressively dissociating man from nature, at least from the old dependence, and that therefore his arts were obliged to take a similar course. Atonality and seriality were not just wilful contradictions of the natural law of sound but deliberate escape routes necessitated by a completely new relationship between man and nature. Indeed, it can be argued that only by dissociation from natural determinism through science and technology can man ultimately hope to survive, even if they also constitute the means, if not the likelihood, of his self-destruction. The matter is complex and cannot be dealt with in detail here; but the fundamentals need to be understood.

For Sibelius it was analysis of and confrontation with the hostile forces of nature that was central. The sense of the human spirit in a hostile waste of desolation becomes the final resolution of *Tapiola.* The sound of his orchestra is hard, dense, unyielding; the sonic equivalent at its most

---

*See Ernest Ansermet's *Les fondements de la musique dans la conscience humaine,* condensed onto record as *What Everyone Should Know About Music* (Decca SXL6131). Ansermet has some pertinent things to say but rather misses the point about avant-garde music by entanglements over *notes* and *sounds* and between *intellect* and *emotion.*

characteristic of the texture of granite. Even at its most congenial, it tends to be ominous; the threat ever present. The forest gods of *Tapiola,* "brooding savage dreams," originate in the Freudian snake pit of the unconscious . The experience of *Tapiola* is frightening precisely because it unlocks forces the civilized mind prefers either to ignore or to explain away. But they can neither be explained away nor ignored. They are the modern form of Fate; they have to be confronted or they will destroy us and our world. They may destroy us in any case; but at least if they are unleashed they can be identified and perhaps tamed. This lies at the centre of the music of Sibelius, its sound and its existential relevance. If it had not been for those forest gods, those brooding figures of the collective unconscious, Sibelius might have become a comparatively genial composer, with the geniality of the Violin Concerto or the opening of the Third Symphony paramount; as genial at bottom as Brahms, though not perhaps as genial as Grieg. But it did not work out that way: he saw deeper and could not evade what he saw. The savage dream haunted him. The sound and texture of his orchestra cannot in the end relent.

Appendix

Recommended Recordings

Sibelius was the first major composer whose reputation outside his own country (and pre-1914 Germany) was substantially created by the gramophone. The sponsoring of recordings of the first two symphonies under Robert Kajanus by the Finnish government in 1930 and the formation of the Sibelius Society by Walter Legge and HMV a year or two later, did more than anything to propogate the gospel of Jean Sibelius, most notably in England and America. There were also other contemporary recordings, some of which like the Schneevoigt Fourth Symphony have only come to light in recent years (this is now available on a disc which also contains the first ever recording of *Luonnotar*).

To the end of his long life Sibelius took an active interest in recordings of his music and maintained a close relationship with his leading interpreters, among them Sir Thomas Beecham, Eugene Ormandy and Basil Cameron, as well as with the younger generation as represented by Tauno Hannikainen. Thereafter, despite the critical collapse of his reputation for a number of years, recordings of Sibelius's music continued to appear with regularity.

The first complete Sibelius cycle came from the late Anthony Collins with the London Symphony Orchestra on Decca. These are still in the catalogue in one form or another and retain a considerable measure of their initial attraction, though the sound, of early LP vintage, does seem a little thin by today's standards. Lorin Maazel made a cycle with the Vienna Philharmonic, also for Decca, during the 1960s and early 1970s, which is more successful in the earlier works; and Sir Colin Davis has made an even better cycle for Philips with the Boston Symphony. Sir John Barbirolli and Paavo Berglund each recorded a cycle for HMV, while Bernstein has recorded all, and Karajan has recorded most of the symphonies. Several conductors have recorded some of the symphonies without embarking upon a full cycle or declaring a particular allegiance to Sibelius's cause.

As much applies to the most popular of the tone poems, which have also been frequently recorded, whether in collections or as "fillups" to the symphonies. And this constitutes a problem. With the exception of the First and Second (and not always with them), Sibelius's symphonies do not offer the convenience of occupying two full LP sides; yet some are not easily accommodated on one side. it is thus necessary in the case of those symphonies which do not, for one reason or another, go readily onto one side but must spread over onto a second, to have something to fill the empty spaces. The obvious solution, and the one invariably taken, is to resort to one or more of the tone poems. This is suitability for the record companies and the artists concerned, but it is not so helpful for the collector and record buyer since it inevitably entails a good deal of superfluous duplication. And this is further aggravated by the familiar determination of both companies and conductors to use a handful of the most popular and frequently recorded pieces for the purpose, so that the record collector in search of some different versions of the symphonies is likely to end up with countless recordings of *Finlandia, Valse triste, The Swan of Tuonela* or *Pohjola's Daughter,* all excellent pieces but not repeatable until the end of time.

Convenience and economy are best served when symphonies occupy either two complete sides or one single side each. This often does happen; but it too can have its perils. It is likely that Collins's unacceptably fast speed (which tended to set a fashion) in the middle movement of the Third Symphony was dictated in part at least by the desire to accommodate the work on a single LP side in the days when cutting techniques were less sophisticated than they subsequently became. Fortunately, the Seventh Symphony has always been able to be fitted onto one LP side, mono or stereo—otherwise it would hardly be possible to record it at all today. (It was of course recorded on the old 78rpm format, with many side breaks, not at all to its advantage; but ironically the greatest of all Sibelius Sevenths, the Society one by Koussevitzky, came originally in that form.)

There are few problems of editions with the works of Sibelius; for, despite his frequent revisions of the scores, authenticity is concerned primarily with matters of style and execution: A few details have been cleared up, as with the revised edition of the Seventh Symphony as recorded by Berglund. But these amount to little more than dynamics and phrasing. The very end of the Second Symphony is a somewhat different matter. The standard Breitkopf & Härtel edition has plain tonic-dominant tympani rolls, used by many conductors, including Colin Davis; but there is an amended version which has repeated notes echoing the end of the chorale theme. This possibly stems from Koussevitzky, who used it, as did Collins and Sir Malcolm Sargent. Berglund makes the best of both worlds by imaginative accentuation.

The following analysis of Sibelius recordings is divided into two parts, the first historical, the second contemporary. The division is not clear cut; but generally speaking the historical refers to those made before 1939, mostly by interpreters closely associated with Sibelius in the days before the evolution of LP (though subsequently transferred), the contemporary, to those made in the LP stereo era, often, but not exclusively, by the second and third generations of Sibelius interpreters. Even though they are all in mono and sound somewhat venerable by today's standards, the historical recordings are irreplaceable. In most cases the transfers have been so expertly done by Anthony Griffiths for World Records that nearly all the artistic merit is preserved. And that merit is indispensable. No understanding of Sibelius and his interpretation is possible without recourse to these historic documents which either exemplify his own specific intentions in regard to his music or deviate from it in ways hardly less illuminating (as in the case of the Schneevoigt versions). Unlike Elgar, though he frequently conducted his music during the active years of his career, with one tiny exception he never made records of it. But he was in the habit of listening to and commenting upon other people's recordings, so that when he gave his stamp of personal approval, he knew what he was talking about and meant what he said.

Inevitably, with a much recorded composer like Sibelius—and recordings continued to appear even during the lowest ebb of his critical reputation—outright recommendations are difficult, dogmatic assertions unacceptable, and usually undesirable: personal preference is bound to play its role, even if critical honesty requires that it be kept under as firm a control as possible. The criteria, as always, must be

a) A standard of interpretation in good style and with some particular insight.

b) Accomplished technical execution on the part of the performers.

c) A high standard of recording quality commensurate with the date of the original recording and its transfer to LP in the case of older versions of high artistic merit. Current catalogue availability is not decisive, if only because what is not available today may well return tomorrow, possibly at a lower price. Additions, deletions and reissues play perpetual havoc with the discographer's best intentions and determinations.

Couplings, where appropriate, are indicated in brackets beneath the main entry. All records are 12″ stereo disc and/or cassette tape (numerated after the disc number where relevant). In the case of pre-stereo recordings, this is designated (M)–mono. Where two or more discs are issued as a set and are not available separately, this is indicated by (nas) after the set or album number.

Historical

Symphony No.1 in E minor Op.39
Kajanus - Symphony Orchestra/London Symphony Orchestra
   (*Belshazzar's Feast* Op.51) World Records SH 191/1 (M) (nas)

Symphony No.2 in D Op.43
Kajanus - Symphony Orchestra/London Symphony Orchestra
   (*Tapiola*) World Records SH191/2 (M) (nas)

Symphony No.3 in C Op.52
Kajanus - London Symphony Orchestra
   (Symphony No.5) World Records SH173/4 (M) (nas)

Symphony No.4 in A minor Op.63
Beecham - London Philharmonic Orchestra
   (*In Memoriam; The Bard; Return of Lemminkäinen*) World Records
   SH133 (M)
Schneevoigt - Finnish National Orchestra
   (*Luonnotar; The Oceanides* (BBC/Boult) World Records SH237 (M)

Symphony No.5 in E flat Op.82
Kajanus - London Symphony Orchestra
   (Symphony No.3) World Records SH173/4 (M) (nas)

Symphony No.6 (in D minor) Op.104
Schneevoigt - Finnish National Orchestra
   (Symphony No.7; *Pohjola's Daughter* (Koussevitzky/Kajanus) World
   Records SH 173/4 (M) (nas)

Symphony No.7 in C Op.105
Koussevitzky - BBC Symphony Orchestra
   (Symphony No.6 (Schneevoigt); *Pohjola's Daughter* (Kajanus); *Karelia Suite* (Kajanus) World Records SH 173/4 (M) (nas)

Violin Concerto in D Op.47
Heifetz/Beecham - London Philharmonic Orchestra
    (*En Saga; Andante Festivo* (Sibelius) World Records SH207 (M)

String Quartet in D Minor *Voces intimae* Op.56
Budapest String Quartet
    (Instrumental pieces (various) World Records SH285 (M)

*All these recordings are essential for a proper understanding of Sibelius interpreta-
tion, and some—notably Kajanus's Third Symphony, Koussevitzky's Seventh,
Beecham's Fourth, the Budapest's quartet—have seldom been equalled and never
surpassed. No one has paced the first two movements of the Third Symphony as
convincingly as Kajanus; and Koussevitzky achieved an extraordinary intensity in
the Seventh, which comes through despite a quality of sound that remains obstinately
sepulchral from which even Tony Griffith's skill has not been able to rescue it.
Heifetz repeated his marvellous performance of the Violin Concerto in a later, stereo,
recording made in America, but Beecham's partnership was missing.*

    *The enigmatic performances are those by Schneevoigt. His Sixth Symphony is
overpaced and fidgety; his Fourth, made in 1934 but apparently not liked by
Sibelius, is interesting. The contrast between the slow movements and the quick ones
is unusally marked. The scherzo in particular is capricious and wilful while the
first and third movements have a dark brooding quality that is most compelling.
The finale is the letdown—rushed and untidily played. There is a trend nowadays
for preferring Schneevoigt to Kajanus; but in spite of the undoubted interest of his
readings—he took over the Finnish National Orchestra when Kajanus retired—it is
difficult to place him on the same plane as a Sibelius interpreter. The preference seems
a matter of fashionable reaction rather than musical reconsideration. His* Luonnotar *however is outstanding, with Helmi Liukkonen the impressive soprano, and
suggests that Schneevoigt's understanding of Sibelius was by no means shallow or
ineffectual.*

    *All these are pre-1939 recordings. Others from the immediate postwar period
are also valuable but do not legitimately come into the true historical category.*

Contemporary

Symphony No.1 in E minor Op.39
Maazel - Vienna Philharmonic Orchestra
    (*Karelia*) Decca Jubilee JB42 - tape KJBC42; US: London 6375

Bernstein - New York Philharmonic
(*Valse triste*) CBS 61804 - tape 40-61804; US: Columbia M30232
Collins - London Symphony Orchestra
(*Pelléas et Mélisande*) Decca Eclipse ECS581, or Ace of Clubs ACL170 (M)

The freshness and vitalism of Maazel's reading remains undiminished, and the sound is excellent. (It would be challenged by Colin Davis with the Boston Symphony if the sound had been as vivid.) Bernstein, as so often, tends to exaggerate; but his ardent advocacy is infectious. Collins's 1950s version has power and passion, with adequate sound (somewhat better in the mono ACL). Beside these most others are worthy but not riveting.

Symphony No.2 in D Op.43
Szell - Concertgebouw Orchestra
(*Finlandia*) Philips Sequenza 6527 111 - tape 7311 111; US: 835306
Barbirolli - Royal Philharmonic Orchestra
RCA Gold Seal GL25011 - Tape GK25011; US: Quin 7008
Bernstein - New York Philharmonic
CBS Classics 61805 - tape 40-61805; US: Columbia MS7337
Karajan - Berlin Philharmonic
HMV ASD4060 - tape TCC-ASD4060 (Philharmonia Orchestra
HMV Concert Classics SXLP30414 - tape TC-SXLP30414)
Beecham - Royal Philharmonic Orchestra
("A musical Autobiography") World Records SH1001/8 (nas)
Berglund - Bournemouth Symphony Orchestra
HMV ASD3414 - tape TC-ASD3414; US: Angel
Davis - Boston Symphony Orchestra
Philips 9500 141 - tape 7300 518; US: ditto

Szell's classic performance is notable for its taut control and intellectual integrity, only going too far in restraint in the finale which lacks the final degree of melodic expansion. Bernstein again tends to exaggerate; but again provides genuine, not synthetic passion and excitement; Barbirolli's reading also captures the vivid impact of a "live" performance. Beecham's recording actually is from a live performance in 1954, at the Royal Festival Hall, London: it remains one of the few occasions when the magic of a Beecham concert was captured on disc. The reissue of Karajan's 1960 recording is welcome—before he re-recorded the symphony in 1980. The approach, like much of this conductor's Sibelius, tends to be a little more Germanic than some, but without in any way distorting the Sibelian idiom. The Berglund is controversial: if Kajanus with his comparatively brisk tempi is the touchstone, then Berglund with his very slow one for the first movement is probably unacceptable. Yet, after initial resistance, an almost hypnotic effect which can be throroughly compelling. Sibelius would probably not have approved; but there are more ways than one of cooking an egg and even composers are not the final arbiters or infallible pontiffs in the matter.

Of other versions, past or present, of this much-recorded symphony Pierre Monteux was not noted as a Sibelius conductor, but the recording he made for Decca is one of the cleanest and most direct—excellent value at a low price. Perhaps the most chilling version came on an old Mercury disc under Paul Paray. The latest, in spectacular digital sound, comes from Vladimir Ashkenazy on Decca. It has been much praised, and it is certainly enthusiastic; but it is also somewhat wayward and self-indulgent in a style better suited to Tchaikovsky, and thus distorts the Sibelian perspectives. In the "enthusiastic" field Leonard Bernstein is much more authentic.

Symphony No.3 in C Op.52
Davis - Boston Symphony Orchestra
    (Symphony No.6) Philips 9500 142 - tape 7300 519; US: ditto
Berglund - Bournemouth Symphony Orchestra
    (Symphony No.5) HMV Greensleeves ESD7094 - tape TC-ESD7094
Kamu - Helsinki Radio Orchestra
    (*En Saga*) DG Privilege 2535 459 - tape 2530 455
With the Sixth, this is the most difficult Sibelius symphony to bring off. Kajanus remains unsurpassed. Of modern versions Davis's is the most imaginative, Berglund's the springiest with a delightful "bounce" to the opening, so often either rushed or bumbled (Barbirolli/HMV), the proper accentuation missed. Okko Kamu has recorded several Sibelius works. He is clearly a gifted musician who understands Sibelius—his slow movement here catches more of its elusive quality than the Berglund—but his orchestra in this case is not quite first rate. All the same, it is illuminating to hear how a young Finn approaches the old master.

Symphony No.4 in A minor Op.63
Davis - Boston Symphony Orchestra
    (*Tapiola*) Philips 9500 143 - tape 7300 520; US: ditto
Berglund - Finnish Radio Orchestra Symphony
    (*Sallinen;* Mauermusik) Finlandia FA312
Karajan - Berlin Philharmonic Orchestra
    (*Swan of Tuonela*) DG Accolade 2542 128 - tape 3342 128
Berglund has recorded the Fourth twice, Karajan has recorded it three times. The two listed versions represent opposite poles: Berglund bleak and direct, Karajan with a tonal opulence that might be out of keeping with the innermost spirit of the music were it not for the searing intensity of the playing. Karajan has said that the Sibelius Fourth is one of the small handful of works that emotionally exhaust him to conduct, and hearing the record one can understand why. Davis's ending lacks imagination, otherwise it represents another outstanding version. But none quite replaces the pre-war Beecham Society (see "Historical") as interpretation and

performance. Beecham achieved a cold detached quality that remains unique, though again it is not the only way to present this masterpiece.

Of earlier versions a coupling of the Fourth and Fifth symphonies by Ormandy and the Philadelphia Orchestra from the mid-1950s (Philips ABL3084 (M); US: Columbia ML-5045) was immensely impressive, especially in the Fourth. A version by Barbirolli (HMV) had much atmosphere and depth but was marred by some untidy orchestral playing. Maazel's Vienna recording (Decca) is one of the best of his series and an excellent buy at a modest price. Bernstein (CBS) is for once curiously perverse, with an inappropriately lumbering scherzo and a very poor Luonnotar *as coupling. The pairing of the Fourth Symphony and* Tapiola *(Davis and Maazel) is telling.*

Symphony No.5 in E flat Op.82
Bernstein - New York Philharmonic
(*Pohjola's Daughter*) CBS Classics 61808 - tape 40-61808; US: Columbia MS6749
Karajan - Berlin Philharmonic Orchestra
(*Tapiola*) DG (SLPM) 138973 or (*En Saga*) HMV ASD3409 - tape TC-ASD3409; US: Angel
or (Symphony No.7) HMV Concert Classics SXLP30430 - tape TC-SXLP30430
Berglund - Bournemouth Symphony Orchestra
(Symphony No.3) HMV Greensleeves ESD7094 - Tape TC-ESD7094
Hannikäinen - Sinfonia of London
(*Karelia*) HMV SXLP30149

Berglund's is more reliable and authentic than inspired. Bernstein is admirable in both "feel" and execution and particularly successful in realizing Sibelius's scoring (note the bassoon line in the symphony). Karajan has recorded this symphony no less than four times: it clearly means much to him and his search for his own ideal in it is constantly illuminating. The earlier EMI version (reissued as above with the Seventh) has an anomaly in the nonauthentic spacing of the final chords; otherwise it remains a memorable version. All the same, once again no modern conductor, not even Karajan, manages to weld the disparate elements of the first movement into a convincing whole as Kajanus did, or to convey the inexorable sense of movement in so subtle a fashion. And it is movement and integration of apparently contrary elements that mark the distinction of the first section at least of the Fifth Symphony.

Symphony No.6 (in D minor) Op.104
Davis - Boston Symphony Orchestra
(Symphony No.3) Philips 9500 142 - tape 7300 519; US: ditto

Karajan - Berlin Philharmonic Orchestra
   (Symphony No.7) DG Accolade 2542 137 - tape 3342 137; US: ditto
   or (Philharmonia Orchestra - Symphony No.7) Columbia 33CX1341
   (M); US: Angel D-35316
Berglund - Bournemouth Symphony Orchestra
   (*Pohjola's Daughter; Luonnotar* (Taru Valjakka) HMV ASD3155
Bernstein - New York Philharmonic
   (Symphony No.7) CBS Classics 61806 - tape 40-61806;

The Sixth is the most elusive of Sibelius's symphonies and the most likely (with the Third) to fail in performance. It contains subtleties not dreamt of in the casebooks of most conductors; or in those of many critics. Yet along with Luonnotar *and* The Bard *it holds secrets of Sibelius's genius which can only be overlooked at risk of a total misunderstanding of him.*

No recording has captured its particular quality: all fail at some point. Bernstein lacks sufficient refinement; Davis and Berglund, especially, are too literal. Karajan has recorded it twice, and it is he who comes nearest to penetrating its innermost nature. His 1956 Philharmonia version is in some ways preferable to the later Berlin issue, largely because the latter, though no less well played, tends to suffer from under-cutting and a rather wan quality of tone. Beecham recorded the Sixth after the war, and Sibelius himself had a particular liking for it (those who know the old HMV 78s will understand why). Unfortunately, contractual difficulties have prevented it from being included in the invaluable World Records series of historical recordings (though in fact it lies just ouside the strict category) and its copyright owners (RCA) have never rereleased it, perhaps because, on the evidence of the 78s, the sound quality is problematical. Barbirolli (HMV) was mentally as well as physically untidy in his recording; Berglund and Maazel seem to approach theirs from the outside. Collins's was good, in his early LP version (Decca), but the sound is now too little refined to satisfy, though the merits of the performance tend to compensate. But this is a delicately hued work, and quality of sound as well as of performance are required.

Symphony No.7 in C Op.105
Bernstein - New York Philharmonic
   (Symphony No.6) CBS Classics 61806 - tape 40-61806; US: Columbia
Karajan - Berlin Philharmonic Orchestra
   (Symphony No.6) DG Accolade 2542 137 - tape 3342 137; US: ditto
   or (Philharmonia Orchestra - Symphony No.5) HMV Concert Classics SXLP30430 - tape TC-SXLP30430 (7 - (M))
Berglund - Bournemouth Symphony Orchestra
   (*Tapiola; The Oceanides*) HMV ASD2874
Beecham - New York Philharmonic
   US: Columbia ML4086

It is becoming wearisome, but it has again to be said that no modern version of the Seventh Symphony matches up to Koussevitzky's great version made in 1933, recorded live and issued in one of the Society albums. Bernstein was a protégé of Koussevitzky and his version has something of the old one's power and intensity; but not all of it. Karajan's two versions are again characteristic of his profound searchings into Sibelius; and again in a somewhat Germanic style, with generally broad tempi and expansive phrasing (an unkind critic on the appearance of the first, Philharmonia, version was heard to snort "Parsifal!") But as in the earlier instances, the effect is by no means inimical; it could even be held to serve the cause of "deparochializing" Sibelius. Berglund's is required hearing, if only because it incorporates a number of corrections to the Hansen score which slightly modify but do not substantially alter the musical bias. The performance itself is good, but not overwhelming. The Beecham, made in New York in the 1940s makes the 1957 version he made for HMV with the Royal Philharmonic sound curiously tame—a pity, since Beecham at his best was one of the great Sibelius conductors. All the same, the HMV, now coupled with a superb Tapiola *and* The Oceanides *(SXLP 30290 - tape TC-SXLP30290) is certainly not to be overlooked. Maazel (Decca) would come well into the reckoning, if his coupling—a rushed and unidiomatic Fifth Symphony—had been acceptable.*

Kullervo Symphony Op.7
Berglund - Bournemouth Symphony Orchestra/Soloists/Helsinki University Male Voice Choir
    (*Scene with Cranes; Swanwhite*) HMV SLS807(2); US: Angel S3778
An excellent, totally convincing performance, finely recorded. Indispensable.

Violin Concerto in D minor Op.47
Heifetz/Hendl - Chicago Symphony Orchestra
    (*Prokofiev:* Concerto No.2) RCA LSB4048; US:
Neveu/Süsskind - Philharmonia Orchestra
    (in "The Art of Ginette Neveu") HMV RLS739(4) (M) (nas)
Kyung-Wha Chung/Previn - London Symphony Orchestra
    (*Tchaikovsky:* Violin Concerto) Decca SXL6493 - tape KSXC6493; US: London 6710
To hear Heifetz play the opening bars is to throw the entire art of violin playing and the concerto of Sibelius into a totally fresh dimension. The purity of line, intensity of expression and the sheer splendour of tone is unsurpassed and probably unsurpassable. It adds a distinction to the concerto and ultimately vindicates it. The only possible comparison is with the late Ginette Neveu (she was killed in an air crash in 1949, aged 30) whose 1945 recording is a miracle of another kind.

Of modern versions that by Kyung-Wha Chung stands out in a fairly crowded field. The late David Oistrakh recorded it twice, once with Ormandy and the Philadelphia, later with Rozhdestvensky and the Moscow Radio Symphony Orchestra, both magisterial performances but somehow not so compelling as the two Heifetz versions and the Neveu. Zino Francescatti has done it with Bernstein, now coupled with Bernstein's rather bustling account of the Third Symphony; Ida Haendel with Berglund and the Bournemouth orchestra also stand high. But no one can really challenge Heifetz and Neveu: the only real question is whether the prewar mono Heifetz with Beecham or the later, stereo, one from America is to be preferred. The latter is better recorded, though not marvellously, but the former has Beecham's more refined partnership. On the whole, though, the RCA must have it, if only one has to suffice. Kyung-Wha Chung and Previn are of course superbly recorded.

The advantage of Oistrakh's later, HMV/Melodiya version, excellent in itself, is that it also contains two of the Humouresques and items from Belshazzar's Feast. *All six Humouresques can be had by Aaron Rosand on Turnabout TV34182S coupled with the Sixth Symphony of Carl Nielsen, or alternatively by Salvatore Accardo with Sir Colin Davis on Philips 9500 675 - tape 7300 770, coupled with yet another fine version of the concerto.*

TONE POEMS

En Saga; The Swan of Tuonela; Pohjola's Daughter; The Bard; Lemminkäinen's Return/Finlandia; Prelude to *The Tempest; Nightride and Sunrise; The Oceanides; Tapiola*
Boult - London Philharmonic Orchestra
    Pye GGCD305(2) (nas)

En Saga: Finlandia: Nightride and Sunrise; Pohjola's Daughter Op.49
Stein - Orchestre de la Suisse Romande
    Decca SXL6542; US: London 6745

Four Legends Op.22; *Karelia* Suite Op.11
Kamu - Helsinki Radio Orchestra
    DG2530 656 - tape 3300 656; US: ditto

Rakastava Op.14; *Scènes historiques* Op.25 & 66;
Valse lyrique Op.96 No.1
Gibson - Scottish National Orchestra
    RCA RL25051 - tape RK25051

Andante festivo; Canzonetta Op.62a; *Dance Intermezzo* Op.45 No.2; *The*

Dryad Op.45 No.1; *Pan and Echo* Op.53a; Romance in C Op.42; Spring
Song Op.16; *Suite champêtre* Op.98b; *Suite mignon* Op.98a; *Valse romantique*
Op.62b
Groves - Royal Liverpool Philharmonic Orchestra
     HMV ASD3287

Pelléas et Mélisande Op.46; *The Oceanides* Op.73; *Tapiola* Op.112
Beecham - Royal Philharmonic Orchestra
     HMV SXL30197 - tape EXE180; US: Angel S35458
Luonnotar Op.70; *En Saga* Op.9; *Nightride and Sunrise* Op.55; *The Oceanides*
Op.73
Dorati/Jones - London Symphony Orchestra
     HMV ASD2486

*Collections of Sibelius tone poems are numerous and tend to proliferate. The above
listing covers most of the ground apart from fillups to recordings of the symphonies.*
  *Boult's pair of discs first appeared in the late 1950s but still sounds good.
There is also a useful two-disc collection by Gibson and the Scottish National
Orchestra on RCA which contains another good version of* Luonnotar. *Two more
recordings of* Luonnotar *come from Berglund on HMV, coupled with the Sixth
Symphony, and by Elisabeth Söderström with Ashkenazy on Decca, coupled with
the Fourth Symphony; but unfortunately neither symphony recording is a primary
recommendation. However, in one version or another,* Luonnotar *is an absolute
necessity in any Sibelius collection.*
  *The Groves anthology of smaller pieces is not marvellously played but does
contain material not otherwise available. Of other compilations, those by Karajan
(DG) Sir John Barbirolli (HMV) and Berglund (HMV) are valuable; but the
problem of excessive duplication is ever present.*

The Tempest Op.109, Suites 1 & 2; *In Memoriam* Op.59
Groves - Royal Liverpool Philharmonic Orchestra
     HMV ASD2961 - tape TC-ASD2961
Strings Quartet in D Minor Op.56 *Voces intimae*
Fitzwilliam Quartet
     (Delius Quartet) L'Oiseau-Lyre DSL047

WORKS FOR VIOLIN AND PIANO

Four Pieces Op.78; Five Pieces Op.81; Four Compositions Op.115; Three
Compositions Op.116
Yaron/Stipleman
     Finlandia FA301

In no sense major Sibelius; but a useful addition none the less. Good playing and recording. Some of these and other instrumental pieces appear on the reverse of the Budapest Quartet recording (Historical) of the Sibelius quartet.

PIANO WORKS

Kyllikki Op.41; Six Impromptus Op.5; Sonata in F Op.12; Six Finnish Folk Songs (1903)
Tawastsjerna (piano)
    BIS-LP153
Ten Pieces, Op.24; Ten Bagatelles Op.34
Tawaststjerna (Piano)
    BIS-LP169
These are the first two volumes in the projected complete cycle of Sibelius's piano music played by the son of the great Sibelius biographer and scholar.

Sonatinas Op.67; *Kyllikki* Op.41
Gould (piano)
    CBS 76674; US: Columbia
Thirteen Pieces Op.76; Ten Pieces Op.40 No.6; Five Pieces Op,75 Nos.3,5; Five Romantic Pieces Op.101 Nos.2,5; Two Rondos Op.68 No,1; Three Sonatinas Op.67
Laszlo (piano)
    RCA GL42229

SONGS

"Arioso"; "Diamenten på Marsson"; "Den Första Hyssen"; "Flickan kom ifrån sin älsklings möte"; "Höstkväll"; "Kom nu hit"; "Men min Fagel märks dock icke"; "Om Kvällen"; "På Verabdan vid Havet"; "Säf, säf, susa"; "Se'n har jag ej fragat mera"; "Svarta Rosor"; "Vaedet en dröm"; "Varen flyktar hastigt"
Flagstad/Fjeldstadt - London Symphony Orchestra
Flagstad treated these Sibelius songs to the "big" style and the grand manner of her later years. They mostly gain thereby.

Selected writings

Scandinavian literature on Sibelius has always been fairly prolific. For the English-speaking reader it came into the mainstream with Cecil Gray's *Sibelius* (Oxford: Oxford University Press, 1931) and was confirmed by the space devoted to Sibelius in Constant Lambert's *Music Ho!* (London: Faber & Faber, 1933, 1936), both books subsequently revised and reissued. But it really began before that, with Rosa Newmarch's *Jean Sibelius: A Finnish Composer,* published in Leipzig in 1906. Rosa Newmarch subsequently added *Jean Sibelius: A Short History of a Long Friendship,* in 1939. A good deal of Sibelius journalism followed over the years, much of it of value. The most important books to come were Bengt de Törne's *Sibelius: A close-up* (London, Boston, 1937), and Harold Johnson's *Jean Sibelius* (New York, 1959, London, 1960), plus Simon Parmet's more specialized study, *The Symphonies of Sibelius* (London, 1959; original Finnish edition, Helsinki, 1955).

Sibelius scholarship was greatly revised and extended by the researches of Professor Erik Tawaststjerna whose exhaustive study in Swedish original appeared during the late 1960s, with an English translation and revision in the mid-1970s. This is invaluable, and so far the final word. Robert Layton's *Sibelius, Master Musicians* (London: Dent 1965, revised in the light of Tawaststjerna's researches, 1978) is illuminating and a well documented introduction to Sibelius and his music. Also to be recommended is the *Symposium* edited by Gerald Abraham which appeared from the firm of Lindsay Drummond in 1947 and brought to bear a sharper criticism in reaction against the excessive laudations of Gray and Lambert. The text is distributed among a number of contributors, each an acknowledged expert in his or her field. The final chapter of Sibelius's style by David Cherniavsky is worth particular attention.

[For more detailed list of writings on Sibelius, see Bibliography.]

Bibliography

The following is a listing of the principal writings on Sibelius, with particular attention to those available in English. Every Sibelius bibliographer in any context must acknowledge a debt to *Jean Sibelius: An International Bibliography on the Occasion of the Centennial Celebrations, 1965,* compiled by Fred Blum and issued as No.8 of the Detroit Studies in Music Bibliography by Information Service, Inc., Detroit.

BOOKS

Abraham, Gerald., ed. *Sibelius: A Symposium.* London: Lindsay Drummond Ltd., 1947; New York (as *The Music of Sibelius*): W.W. Norton & Co., Inc., 1947. (Reissued by Oxford University Press, London, 1952.)

Arnold, Elliot. *Finlandia: The Story of Sibelius,* Illus. Lolita Granahan. New York: Henry Holt & Co., 1941; rev. ed. 1950.

Downes, Olin. *Sibelius.* Helsinggissä: Kustannusosakeyhtiö Otava, 1945.

——*Sibelius the Symphonist.* New York: The Philharmonic Symphony Society, 1956.

Ekman, Karl. *Jean Sibelius: en konstnärs liv och personlighet.* Stockholm: Bokförlaget Natur och Kultur, 1935. English edition: *Jean Sibelius: His Life and*

Personality (trans. Edward Birse). Helsinki: Holger Schildts Förlag, 1935; London: Alan Wilmer Ltd., 1936; New York: Alfred A. Knopf, 1938.

Gray, Cecil. *Sibelius.* London: Oxford University Press, 1931

——*Sibelius: The Symphonies.* London: Oxford University Press, 1975.

Hannikainen, Ilmari. *Sibelius and the Development of Finnish Music.* Trans. Aulis Nopsanen. London: Hinrichsen Editions Ltd., 1948.

Helasvuo, Veikko. *Sibelius and the Music of Finland.* Helsinki: Otava. London: Francis, Day and Hunter, 1952.

Johnson, Harold E. *Jean Sibelius.* New York: Alfred A. Knopf, 1959; London: Faber & Faber, 1960. (Finnish and Swedish trans.)

——*Jean Sibelius: The Recorded Music.* Helsinki: Oy R.E. Westerlund Ab., 1957.

Layton, Robert. *Sibelius.* London: J.M. Dent & Sons Ltd., 1965, rev. 1978.

Leibowitz, René. *Sibelius, le plus mauvais compositeur du monde.* Liège: Aux Éditions Dynamo, 1955.

Levas, Santeri. *Jean Sibelius: muistelma suuresta ihmisestä.* 2 Vols. Porvoo, Helsinki: Werner Söderström Osakeyhtiö, 1957-60.

——*Sibelius: A Personal Portrait.* London: 1972.

Newmarch, Rosa. *Jean Sibelius: A Finnish Composer.* Leipzig: Brussels; London; New York:Breitkopf & Härtel, 1906.

——*Jean Sibelius: A Short History of a Long Friendship.* Boston: C.C. Birchard Co., 1939; London: Goodwin & Tabb Ltd., 1945.

Niemann, Walter. *Jean Sibelius.* Leipzig: Breitkopf & Härtel, 1917.

Parmet, Simon. *Sibelius symfonier: en studie i musikförstaelse.* Helsinki: Söderström & Co.; Stockholm: Hugo Gebers Förlag, 1955. English edition: *The Symphonies of Sibelius: A Study in Music Appreciation* (trans. Kingsley A. Hart). London: Cassel & Co. Ltd., 1959.

Ringbom, Nils-Eric. *Sibelius.* Helsinki: Holger Schildts Förlag; Stockholm: Albert Bonniers Förlag, 1948.

——*Sibelius: Symfonier, Symfoniska dikter, Vilkonsert, Voces intimae, Analytiska beskrivningar.* Helsinki: Fazers Musikhandel, 1955. English, French, German trans.

Roiha, Eino. *Die Symphonien von Jean Sibelius: eine formanalytische Studie.* Jyväskylä, 1941.

Rosas, John. *Otryckta kammarmusikverk av Jean Sibelius.* Abo: Abo Akademi, 1961.

Salmenhaara, Erkki, and Tirranen, Herta. *Sibelius and Ainola.* Porvoo, Helsinki: 1976.

Sbarcea, George. *Jean Sibelius.* Bucharest: 1965 (In Rumanian).

Schouwman, Hans. *Sibelius.* Haarlem & Antwerp: Gottmer, 1949.

Sibelius, Jean. *Jean Sibelius: Manuscripts.* Helsinki: Oy R.E. Westerland Ab, 1945. (Facsimile reproductions of Sibelius autographs.)

Simlä, Martti. *Sibeliana.* Helsingissä: Kustannusosakeyhtiö Otava, 1945.

Stupel, Aleksandr Moiseevich. *Jean Sibelius, 1865-1957.* Leningrad: Gos. muzykal'noe izd-vo, 1963.

Sugano, Hirokazu. *Sibelius: Life and Work.* Tokyo: 1967. (in Japanese).

Tanzberger, Ernst. *Jean Sibelius: eine Monographie.* Wiesbaden: Breitkopf & Härtel, 1962.

——*Die symphonischen Dictungen von Jean Sibelius (Eine inhalts und formanalytische Studie).* Würzburg: Konrad Triltsch Verlag, 1943.

Tawaststjerna, Erik. *The Pianoforte Compositions of Sibelius.* Helsingssä: Kustannusosakethtiö Otava, 1957.

——*Ton och tolkning: Sibelius-studier.* Helsinki: Holger Schildts Förlag; Stockholm: Wahlström & Widstrand, 1957.

——*Jean Sibelius.* Helsinki - vol 1 (1965); vol.2 (1967); vol.3 (1972); vol.4 (1978). (English and Swedish editions)

Törne, Bengt de. *Sibelius: A Close-Up.* London: Faber & Faber; Boston: Houghton Mifflin Co., 1937. (Swedish, Finnish, Italian trans.)

Vignal, Marc. *Jean Sibelius.* Paris, 1965.

Vachnadze, Margarita Akselevna. *Jean Sibelius.* Moscow: Sovetskii Kompozitor, 1963.

Vestdijk, Simon. *De symfonieën van Jean Sibelius.* Amsterdam: De Bezige Bij; Rotterdam: Nijgh & Van Ditmar, 1962.

The Works of Jean Sibelius. Compiled by Lauri Solanterä for Oy R.E. Westerlund Ab, Helsinki, 1955.

BIOGRAPHIES AND GENERAL BOOKS CONTAINING EXTENSIVE REFERENCES TO SIBELIUS

Bacharach, Alfred Louis. *The Music Masters.* vol.4; London: Cassel & Co., Ltd., 1954, Penguin Books, 1957.

Bakeless, Katherine. *Short Lives of Great Composers.* New York: Stokes, 1940.

Barlow, Wayne. *Foundations of Music.* New York: Appleton-Century-Crofts, 1953.

Barne, Kitty. *Listening to the Orchestra.* London: J.M. Dent & Sons Ltd., 1941.

Bauer, Marion. *Twentieth Century Music; How It Developed, How to Listen to It.* New York: London, Putnam & Co., 1933.

Bax, Arnold. *Farewell My Youth.* London: Longmans, Green & Co. Ltd. 1943.

Bernstein, Martin. *An Introduction to Music.* New York: Prentice-Hall, 1937.

Brockway, Wallace, and Weinstock, Herbert. *Men of Music: Their Lives, Times, and Achievements.* New York: Simon & Schuster, 1939 (rev. 1950).

Brook, Donald. *Composers' Gallery: Biographical Sketches of Contemporary Composers.* London: Rockliff & Co. Ltd., 1946.

Cardus, Neville. *Ten Composers.* London: Jonathan Cape & Co. Ltd., 1945. (See also *A Composer's Eleven,* Cape, 1958, New York: George Braziller & Co., 1958).

Copland, Aaron. *Our New Music: Leading Composers in Europe and America.* New York & London: McGraw-Hill Book Co., 1941.

Demuth, Norman. *An Anthology of Musical Criticism.* London: Eyre & Spottiswoode & Co. Ltd., 1947.

——*Musical Trends in the Twentieth Century.* London: Rockliffe & Co. Ltd., 1952.

Downes, Edward. *Adventures in Symphonic Music.* New York, Toronto: Farrar & Rinehart Co. Inc., 1944.

Downes, Olin. *Olin Downes on Music.* New York: Simon & Schuster, 1957.

Ewen, David. *The Book of Modern Composers.* New York: Alfred A. Knopf Inc., 1942 (*New Book,* 1961).
——*Twentieth Century Composers.* New York: Thomas Y. Cromwell Co., 1937. *The Complete Book of 20th Century Composers.* New York: Prentice-Hall Inc., 1952.
Flodin, Karl Teodor. *Finska musiker och andra uppsatser i musik.* Helsinki: Söderström, 1900.
——*Martin Wegelius: levnadsteckning.* Helsinki: 1922
——*Musikliv och reseminnen.* Helsinki: Söderström, 1931.
Forslin, Alfhild. *Runeberg i musiken: bibliografi med kommentarer och historisk översikt.* Helsinki: Svenska Litteratursällskapet i Finland, 1958.
Foulds, John. *Music Today: Its Heritage from the Past, and Legacy to the Future.* London: Nicholson & Watson Ltd., 1934.
Frosterus, Sigurd. *Stalalderns Janusansikte och andra essäer.* Helsinki, Stockholm: Schildt, 1935.
Gavazzeni, Gianändrea. *Musicisti d'Europa: studi sui contemporanei.* Milan: Suvini Zerboni, 1954.
Gilman, Lawrence. *Toscanini and Great Music.* New York, Toronto: Farrar Inc., 1938.
Goossens, Eugene. *Overture and Beginners: A Musical Autobiography.* London: Methuen & Co. Ltd., 1951.
Grey, Cecil. *A Survey of Contemporary Music.* London: Oxford University Press, 1924.
——*Predicaments, or Music and the Future: An Essay in Constructive Criticism.* London: Oxford University Press, 1936.
Grout, Donald Jay. *A History of Western Music.* New York: Norton & Co. Inc., 1960.
Haapanen, Toivo. *La musique finlandaise.* Paris: Société française d'imprimerie et de librairie, 1924.
——*Suomen säveltaide.* Helsingissä: Otava, 1940.
Halonen, Antti. *Taiteen juhlaa ja arkea,* Helsinki: Tammi, 1952.
Hartog, Howard (ed). *European Music in the Twentieth Century.* London: Routledge and Kegan Paul, 1957; New York, Praeger, 1957.
James, Burnett. *An Adventure in Music.* London: John Baker Ltd., 1967.
Johnson, Harold Earle. *Symphony Hall, Boston.* Boston: Little, Brown Co., 1950.
Kakinuma, Tarō. *Kindai ongaku kanshō.* Tokyo: Ongaku no Tomo Sha, 1953.
Karvonen, Arvi. Sibelius-Akatemia 75 vuotta. Helsinki: Otava, 1957.
Klemetti, Heikki. *Piirteitä Suomen musiikin historiasta.* Porvoo, Helsinki: Söderström, 1919.
Krohn, Ilmari. *Sävelmusstoja elämäni varrelta.* Porvoo, Helsinki: Söderström, 1951.
——*Kulttuurin saavutuksia, suomalaisten tiedemiesten ja taiteilijain esitämänä.* Porvoo, Helsinki: Söderström, 1946.
Lambert, Constant. *Music Ho!: A Study of Music in Decline.* London: Faber & Faber, 1933 (rev. ed., 1936); New York: Scribner, 1934.
Landowska, Wanda. *Histoire de la musique moderne. (1900-1940)* Aubier: Editions Montaigne, 1941.

Leichtenritt, Hugo. *Music of the Western Nations.* Cambridge, Mass.: Harvard University Press, 1938.

Maasalo, Kai. *Suuri sinfoniamusiikki, Haydnista Sibeliukseen.* Porvoo, Helsinki: Söderström, 1956.

Mellers, Wilfred. *Man and His Music, vol.4.* London, Barrie & Rockliff Ltd., 1962; Fair Lawn, N.J.: Essential Books, 1967.

Myers, Rollo H. (ed.). *Twentieth Century Music.* London, John Calder Ltd., 1960.

Newman, Ernest. *From the World of Music: Essays from the* "Sunday Times". London: John Calder Ltd., 1956; New York, Coward-McCann Inc.

——*More Essays from the World of Music.* London: John Calder Ltd. 1958; New York: Coward-McCann Inc.

Norgard, Per. *Sibelius og Danmark.* Suomen Musiikin Vuosirkirja, 1965.

Parmet, Simon. *Con amore: essäer om musik och mästare.* Helsinki: Söderström, 1960.

Pergament, Moses. *Ny Vandring med Fru Musica.* Stockholm: Norstedt, 1944.

——*Vandring med Fru Musica.* Stockholm: Norstedt, 1943.

Ranta, Sulho. *Musiikin valtateillä: musiikkia ja muusikoita.* Porvoo, Helsinki: Söderström, 1942.

Ringbom, Nils-Eric. *Helsingfors Orkesterföretag, 1882-1932.* Helsinki: Suomentanut Taneli Kuusisto, 1932.

Rosenfeld, Paul, *Musical Portraits: Interpretations of Twenty Modern Composers.* New York: Harcourt, Brace and Howe, 1920.

Rothery, Agnes. *Finland: The New Nation.* New York: Viking Press Inc., 1936.

Samminsky, Lazare. *Music of Our Day: Essentials and Prophetics.* New York: Thomas Y. Crowell Inc., 1939.

Schiller, Harald. *Thalia i Malmö och andra essayer.* Malmö: Sydsvenska Dagbladets a-b, 1948.

Schnittkind, Henry Thomas & Dana Arnold. *Forty Famous Composers.* New York: Halcyon House, 1948.

Soegmeister, Elie (ed.). *The Music Lover's Handbook.* New York: William Morrow & Co. Inc., 1943.

Slonimsky, Nicolas. *Music Since 1900.* New York: Norton & Co. Inc., 1937.

Soderhjelm, Werner (ed.). *Finlande et Finlandais.* Paris: Librairie Armand Colin, 1913.

Simpson, Robert. *Sibelius and Nielsen.* London: BBC, 1965.

Thompson, Oscar. (ed.). *Great Modern Composers.* New York: Dodd, Mead & Co. Inc., 1941.

Thomson, Virgil. *The Music Scene.* New York: Alfred Knopf Inc., 1945.

Ulrich, Homer. *Symphonic Music: Its Evolution Since the Renaissance.* New York: Columbia University Press, 1952.

Wegelius, Martin. *Länsimaisen musiikin historia pääpiirt-eissään.* Helsinki: K.E. Holm, 1904.

Wood, Henry J. *My Life of Music.* London: Victor Gollancz Ltd., 1938.

Wuolijoki, Sulo. *Hämettä ja hämäläisiä.* Helsinki: Oy Suomen kirja, 1945.

TECHNICAL AND ANALYTICAL VOLUMES

Balgar, Robert C & Biancolli, Louis. *The Concert Companion: A Comprehensive Guide to Symphonic Music.* New York: London, McGraw-Hill Co., 1947.

Biancolli, Louis (ed.). *The Analytical Concert Guide.* New York: Doubleday & Co. Inc., 1951.

Brodin, Gereon. *En värld av musik: en orientering i den symfoniska konsertrepertoaren.* Stockholm: Nordisk Rotogravyr, 1954.

Ferguson, Donald. *Masterworks of the Orchestra Repertoire: A Guide for Listeners.* Minneapolis: University of Minneapolis Press, 1954.

Flor, Kai. *Symfonibogen.* Knøbenhavn: Det Schønbergske Forlag, 1947.

Gilman, Lawrence. *Orchestral Music: An Armchair Guide.* New York: Oxford University Press Inc., 1951.

Hill, Ralph (ed.). *The Symphony.* London: Penguin Books, 1949.

Newmarch, Rosa. *Jean Sibelius: Vierte Symphonie.* Leipzig: Breikopf & Härtel, 1913.

O'Connell, Charles. *The Victor Book of the Symphony.* New York: Simon & Schuster, 1941.

Seaman, Julian. *Great Orchestral Music: A Treasury of Program Notes.* New York: Toronto, Rinehart & Co. Inc., 1950.

Simpson, Robert, ed. *The Symphony.* London: Penguin Books, 1965.

Spaeth, Sigmund Gottfried. *A Guide to Great Orchestral Music.* New York: Modern Library, 1943.

Tovey, Donald Francis. *Essays in Musical Analysis, 1-6.* London: Oxford University Press, 1936-39.

Westermann, Gerhart von. *Knaurs Konzertführer.* Munich: Verlagsanstalt, 1951; London, Thames & Hudson Ltd., 1963 (as *Concert Guide*).

Index of Sibelius's Works

Miscellaneous Orchestral Music

Chamber Music

Theatre Music (Incidental)

Songs, Operas and Choral

General Index